Jesus vs. Jihad

Jesus vs. Jihad

Marvin Yakos

Charisma®
HOUSE
Books about Spirit-Led Living

Jesus vs. Jihad by Marvin Yakos
Published by Charisma House
A part of Strang Communications Company
600 Rinehart Road
Lake Mary, Florida 32746
www.charismahouse.com

Unless otherwise noted, all Scripture quotations are from the New King James Version. Copyright © 1979, 1980, 1982 by Thomas Nelson, Inc., publishers. Used by permission.

Verses from the Qur'an quoted in this book are from various translations, but mostly from *The Holy Qur'an*, English Translation of the Meanings of the Qur'an with Notes by Abdullah Yusuf Ali (Indianapolis, IN: H & C International, 1992) and *The Koran*, translated by N. J. Dawood (Penguin Classics, 1990).

Library of Congress Catalog Card Number: 2001097026
International Standard Book Number: 0-88419-880-4

Portions of this book were originally published as *Jesus vs. Jihad*, ISBN 1-877717-06-1, by Accord Books, a part of Strang Communications Company, copyright © 1990.

01 02 03 04   87654321
Printed in the United States of America

I would like to dedicate this book to all those who lost loved ones on September 11, 2001, and to everyone who has given of themselves to help their fellow man.

He was in the world, and the world was made through Him, and the world did not know Him. He came to His own, and His own did not receive Him. But as many as received Him, to them He gave the right to become children of God, to those that believe in His name.

—JOHN 1:10–12

ACKNOWLEDGMENTS

Terror and death threaten all who disagree with or oppose the sacred rage of fundamental Islam. This book can't go forth without a tremendous acclaim for the missionaries that selflessly work for Jesus in Islamic countries. They look persecution and death in the eye daily. Many are killed. We must pray for them daily.

I thank those who helped make this book possible, though unfortunately and for obvious reasons, they must remain unnamed. Thanks to Marlene. Thanks to my mentor Ed Mason, Ph.D., for his support and encouragement. Above all, thanks to Jesus who continues to shine a light on my path.

Contents

Introduction

Open rebuke is better than love carefully concealed.
—Proverbs 27:5

O f foremost concern, this book is not intended to offend or condemn anyone, especially Arabs or our Muslim brothers and sisters. We strive only to present truth. We realize that there are many Muslims who do not agree with the barbaric killing perpetrated in the name of Allah and his prophet Muhammad. We wish to acknowledge the fact that not all Muslims adhere to the radical fundamental dogmas of the Qur'an, but have a wide range of beliefs. Most Muslims in no way strive to terrorize or kill anyone.

We do, however, openly rebuke Satan, his minions and his diabolic methods. We attack spiritual bondage, ignorance, arrogance, persecution, terrorism, murder and lies. Jesus dearly loves the Muslims, as well as Osama bin Laden and his fellow terrorists. We, as followers of Jesus, are also commanded to love them. We only assail that which would destroy them. We view Islamic moderation as a ray of hope and violent *jihad* as having satanic aspirations.

The terrorism that stems from the Middle East and has reached American shores gives the world an intimate glimpse into the true nature of the Qur'an. Travel in Islamic countries is limited and has become increasingly dangerous for anyone other than a Muslim. To understand why, we will dive beneath the peripheral bedlam and thin veneer of pervasive, noneffectual humanism to examine a dilemma that underlies these seething political ideologies.

Qur'anic decrees stem from a deadly and fervent spiritual war with ancient roots and eternal implications. The ever-growing tide of fundamental terrorism and its destructive policies can no longer be met with bland theories, false idealistic hopes, superficial watered-down realizations or Band-Aid solutions. The Qur'anic message must be seen and understood for what it really is.

> For we do not wrestle against flesh and blood, but against principalities and powers, *against the rulers of the darkness of this age*, against spiritual hosts of wickedness in the heavenly places.
> —EPHESIANS 6:12, EMPHASIS ADDED

The Word of God admonishes, "And have no fellowship with the unfruitful works of darkness, *but rather expose them*" (Eph. 5:11, emphasis added).

Jesus is God incarnate. The Qur'an claims He is not. All Islamic principles are built on this most basic premise. The Qur'an has one major goal: to darken the world and to remove any link to its only Savior, Jesus Christ. *Jesus vs. Jihad* pits the Word of God, the Bible, against the surge and onslaught of fundamental Islam and penetrates to the very heart of the matter.

The necessary weaponry must be used to separate

truth from falsehood. Jesus provides such a weapon. It is His Word, the double-edged sword of truth. Jesus did not come with the attitude of "live and let live," an attitude that has become popular in many of today's humanistic and fear-stricken religions of convenience. He came to destroy the works of the devil (1 John 3:8).

In Matthew 10:34, Jesus said, "Do not think that I came to bring peace on earth. I did not come to bring peace but a sword."

Not to be misconstrued, this sword of truth is not a cold, physical blade of steel, but the very Word of God. His Word can expose and destroy Satan's Islamic plan. It can withstand all things. It will last forever. Jesus said, "Heaven and earth will pass away, but My words will by no means pass away" (Matt. 24:35).

We hope and pray this exposé will find favor in the hearts of those who sincerely seek truth. Again, we pray and strive to offend no one. By virtue of truth itself, we pray that someone bound by the evil we expose will realize and seek truth. "The Lord is not slack concerning His promise, as some count slackness, but is longsuffering towards us, not willing that any should perish but that all should come to repentance" (2 Pet. 3:9).

According to the Holy Bible, God came to earth as the supreme sacrifice so that we might gain eternal life. The revelation of Jesus as God is what we wish to convey to all men, to all Muslims. Within Jesus one can find God. Jesus is the real Allah.

> For in Him dwells all the fullness of the Godhead bodily; and you are complete in Him, who is the head of all principality and power.
> —COLOSSIANS 2:9–10

Muhammad claimed that Islam is a superior religion, the final word. He claimed it lines up with previous scripture. But under the alias of Allah, murder and mayhem are recommended, even encouraged. This book will show that Islam in no way aligns with Scripture, but rather distorts it. It is written, "Lest Satan should take advantage of us; for we are not ignorant of his devices" (2 Cor. 2:11).

The radical, fundamentalist terrorist warns, "Keep quiet or die!" It is no surprise that Satan will strike when his ways are probed or a light is shone upon his deeds. A rat is most threatening when cornered. When a rock is lifted and light shines on a poisonous snake, it will strike. Satan is such a snake, the serpent of old.

Jesus showed us how to love our enemies. He took every insult, every accusation and every inhumane blow from time immemorial upon Himself. He loved and forgave those who brutally killed Him. Though He could have called legions of angels from heaven, He voiced no hostility, but continued to love His enemies. He simply said, "Father, forgive them, for they do not know what they do" (Luke 23:34).

To those who did not believe in Him, Jesus said:

> You are of your father the devil, and the desires of your father you want to do. He was a murderer from the beginning, and does not stand in the truth, because there is no truth in him. When he speaks a lie, he speaks from his own resources, for he is a liar and the father of it. But because I tell you the truth, you do not believe Me.
>
> —JOHN 8:44–45

A popular Islamic adage claims that Jesus and Muhammad are brothers in heaven. But when we read their respective scriptures, we find that they are not brothers—not in heaven or anywhere else. Their creeds are not even remotely related; rather, they are diametrically opposed. We cannot accept Islam as truth. As Paul wrote to the Christians at Ephesus, "Nor give place to the devil" (Eph. 4:27).

1

Antichrist

As you have heard that the Antichrist is coming, even now many antichrists have come, by which we know that it is the last hour.

—1 JOHN 2:18

S carcely a decimal point into the new millennium, on September 11, 2001, life, as the entire free world knew it, changed forever. An age-old adversary unexpectedly reared its hideous head and vowed to destroy all we hold dear, including our freedom to choose Jesus Christ as Savior. No matter the hollow overtures of peace, Islam is a religion of antichrist and will play a significant role in the End-Times scenario. As we shall learn, Islam denies the deity of Jesus, negates the cross and is intent on the annihilation of all Christians and Jews.

> *Who is a liar but he who denies that Jesus is the Christ?* He *is antichrist who denies the Father and the Son.* Whoever denies the Son does not have the Father either; he who acknowledges the Son has the Father also.
>
> —1 JOHN 2:22–23, EMPHASIS ADDED

The darker, evil side of Islam invaded America's shores and achieved murderous triumph. The impenetrable curtain between East and West was torn with sürahs (chapters) from the Qur'an boldly manifested in fire, smoke, death and pure unadulterated terror. The fundamentalist Muslim terrorist, no doubt, is ignorantly celebrating the damage caused by his so-called righteous, noble and sacrificial actions. For a brief moment he has been able to drown out the cries of his own empty soul.

There are many questions we must ask. What motivates a Muslim man to surrender his life in such unspeakable and senseless acts of murder and mayhem? What is the root cause of this evil that has entered our shores? What is this evil spirit's ultimate goal? How are we to proceed? How do we stop them? As the Bible admonishes, we will test these spirits to see if they are of God, and we will not be ignorant of their devices. (See 2 Corinthians 2:11; 1 John 4:1.)

Islam's topmost goal, as set forth in the Qur'an and Hadith (Islamic written traditions), is to bring all of mankind into submission to Allah. Imitating Muhammad's example, the religion of Islam is the driving force behind most terrorist acts today. Muhammad hated the Jews more than anyone. America is protecting Israel, and according to the Qur'an, America must be eliminated. Adherents to the Qur'an are to kill or enslave all infidels, or unbelievers, to the dictates of Allah and Muhammad his Prophet (Sürah 2:190–192; 4:76; 5:33; 9:5, 29, 41; 47:4).

Muhammad declared, "The last hour will not come before the Muslims fight the Jews and the Muslims kill them all."[1]

The Hadith suggests that sending the prophet Muhammad with the final message was itself one of the signs of the final hour. It also suggests that there will be no other prophet between Muhammad and the coming of the final hour, which the Hadith says is coming near. The prophet Muhammad composed the following two verses:

I have been commanded to fight against (the Unbelieving) people, till they testify to the fact that there is no God but Allah, and believe in me (Muhammad) as the Messenger from the Lord, and when they do it, their blood and riches are guaranteed protection on my behalf except where it is justified by law.

—HADITH

The Last Hour would not come unless the Muslims fight against the Jews and the Muslims will pursue them until the Jews hide themselves behind a stone or a tree and a stone or tree would say: "Muslim, or the servant of Allah, there is a Jew behind me. Come and kill him."

—SAHIH MUSLIM BOOK 40, NO. 6985

Jihad, which is translated as holy war or effort, is treachery masquerading as truth, fueled only by evil men, doing evil things, to little purpose but to inflict suffering and cause death to generally innocent people. Will such actions heal a Muslim's heart? No, the heart will just get more empty and dead, and so the ideological rhetoric will have to be shouted a little more loudly next time to drown out the self-witness to subhuman character. Terrorist atrocities are at best anesthesia for cold, empty hearts, for they certainly do not accomplish their so-called ideological aim of peace.

Wicked spiritual devices initiate terrorism, but it is the emptiness of the soul that always precedes its reprehensible manifested works. The ignorant and unimportant Muslim is promised an immediate trip to heaven if he commits suicide and kills unbelievers. As such, he is vaulted into prominence as a holy warrior, a martyr for righteousness and a punisher of the wicked.

Osama bin Laden is only one among numerous enraged men exhibiting the personification and directives of a terribly evil spirit. More Muslims than the world would like to admit revere him, because what he did falls in line with what the Qur'an teaches. Whether the Muslims are willing to fight in *jihad* or not, many admire him because he successfully attacked what the Ayatollah Khomeini referred to as the "big Satan" and exposed America's vulnerability. It's time to wake up! Unmistakably, we must understand Islam as it is.

Osama bin Laden's abominable, inhuman actions were designed to terrorize America, to make her lose heart, to destroy her spirit of freedom. His desire is to kill all Americans and freedom-loving peoples. But his deepest and all-consuming intent is to inflame and unite the entire Islamic world in the holy war called *jihad*. His actions are now immortalized in brutal reality and his rhetoric whispered along Islamic corridors. On the streets, most fundamentalist Muslims celebrate and gleefully agree.

> For the Unbelievers Allah hath prepared a humiliating punishment.
>
> —SŪRAH 4:102

> Then those who reject Faith in the Signs of Allah will suffer the severest penalty, and Allah is Exalted in Might, Lord of Retribution.
>
> —SŪRAH 3:4

> Those who reject the Book and the (revelations) with which We sent Our apostles: But soon shall they know—when the yokes (shall be) round their necks, and the chains; they shall be dragged along—in the boiling fetid fluid, then in the Fire shall they be burned.
>
> —SŪRAH 40:70–72

During the first stages of the war on terrorism, Osama bin Laden and his warriors hid themselves in caves. They should get some practice. There may not be enough caves on earth to house them when Jesus returns. In Isaiah 2:19 we read, "They shall go into the holes of the rocks, and into the caves of the earth, from the terror of the LORD and the glory of His majesty, when He arises to the shake the earth mightily."

Sheik Abu Hamza said of the World Trade Center destruction from the safety of his London mosque, "Many people will be happy, jumping up and down at this moment."

The Associated Press reported that Osama bin Laden in a videotaped interview praised Allah for the Twin Towers terrorist attacks and swore America would never dream of security until the infidel armies leave the lands of Muhammad. He said, "America was hit by Allah in one of its softest spots. America is full of fear from its north to its south, from its west to its east. Thank Allah for that. The war against Afghanistan and Osama bin Laden is a war on Islam."

Terror struck into the hearts of an enemy is not only a means; it is the end in itself. Once a condition of terror is obtained in an opponent's heart, there is hardly anything left to be achieved. It is the point where the means and the end merge. *Terror is not a means of imposing a decision upon the enemy; it is the decision the terrorist wishes to impose upon him.* Terrorism is designed not only to make its recipient retreat, but also to destroy his confidence. Terror can be instilled only if the opponent's faith is destroyed. But Jesus has provided Christians with the shield of faith, which no terror can penetrate. To instill terror into the hearts of the enemy, it is essential, in the ultimate analysis, to dislocate his faith.[2]

As the plot sickens, consider the mood in the cockpit of United Airlines flight 11 just before it hit the first tower of the World Trade Center. Were minions of evil spirits in full possession of the terrorists with many thousands more ecstatically screeching? Did the terrorists hold the controls steady? As the second group of terrorists approached the World Trade Center on their ill-fated United Airlines flight 175 and saw the first tower burning, what went through their minds? Were they breathing hard? Were they frightened? Did they scream *jihad*? Did they simply smile a crooked smile? Were they shaky, or did their faith in Allah and his promises of immediate paradise hold them steady at the controls? *Jihad*, holy war—we must ask, "What is holy about it?"

The Lord prospered America above all nations, for we were first formed on biblical principles. Yet, we've persisted in worshiping idols of every dominion. God has endured our shameless sensuality, our mockery of holy things, our shedding of innocent blood and our tireless efforts to remove Him from our society. Now the time has run out, unless we again find God as a nation.

Throughout the Book of Isaiah God said through the prophet, "I've sent you prophet after prophet, watchman after watchman. You've been warned again and again. Yet still you won't open your eyes to your wicked ways. Now I've stricken you, in hopes of saving you. I want to heal your land, to destroy your enemies, to bring you back into My blessing. But you don't have eyes to see it."

What will be America's fate if we reject God's call to turn back to Him? Will we put our trust solely in mankind to see us through? Do we rely on our armed might rather than on God for power? Should we now inscribe on our currency, "In Man We Trust"? Isaiah describes what happens to every nation that rejects God and boasts of its own greatness:

> They shall mount up like rising smoke. Through the wrath of the LORD of hosts the land is burned up, and the people shall be as fuel for the fire.
>
> —ISAIAH 9:18–19

The free world needs to understand that the ultimate goal of Islam is to establish the absolute and uncompromising rule of Allah on earth. The Qur'an mentions peace often, but the peace spoken of occurs only for Muslims. According to the Qur'an, lasting peace will come only when there are no more unbelievers. Under the guise of this one-sided, so-called peace, we find only loss of our God-given inalienable freedoms, loss of free will, bloodlust and the debauchery of women. Muslims have no freedom outside of Islam. They are not allowed to read the Bible under penalty of death. Only the Qur'an and Muhammad's dictates are allowed. Loss of free will leads to arrogance and ignorance, and when ignorance and arrogance unite, fanaticism is born. The Qur'an commands Muslims to wage war against all non-Muslims.

> Seize them and slay them wherever ye find them: and (in any case) take no friends or helpers from their ranks.
> —SŪRAH 4:89

> Allah hath granted a grade higher to those who strive and fight with their goods and persons than to those who sit (at home).
> —SŪRAH 4:95

In the Middle East, where Americans recently died protecting Islamic nations during the Gulf War, there is a total blackout on anything Christian. One cannot carry a Bible on the street or have a Bible study in the privacy of one's own home. Even at American embassies, over which the American flag flies, Christian church services are banned. A convert to Christianity or any other religion from Islam faces the death penalty in Muslim countries. As far as most Muslims are concerned, they were born Muslim and they will die Muslim. This philosophy is drummed into them from childhood.

7

Only Muslims can be citizens in most Muslim countries. Even in countries where the government does not enforce Islamic law, Islam's influence prevents freedom of speech, the press, religion and conscience. In territories belonging to the Palestinian Liberation Organization (PLO), Christian Arabs who once had freedom under Israel now suffer persecution, imprisonment and death for their faith. Muslims build mosques and worship freely in the West, but in their own countries they deny such freedoms to others. Instead of reporting such hypocrisy, the media, mismanaged with clever political skill, cover it up.

As terror and darkness continue to spread, the proliferating spirits of Allah continue to devour humanity, 25 percent at present and growing faster than any religion on earth. Imagine this spirit unchecked and bin Laden in a world that is 75 percent Muslim. Imagine Allah's will imposed on the entire world. Would the unbeliever still hear overtures of peace? How many of us realize that the Qur'an instructs Muslims to make friends with their enemies, advocate peace if they are too weak to attack, and then let their enemies feed them until they are strong enough to kill them?

Perhaps for many this evolving scenario is all too much. Perhaps it is too shocking and disturbing to even contemplate. It just doesn't fit into the American dream of "live and let live." Perhaps a person is not quite sure which spirit is which, or perhaps he believes that all spiritual roads lead to the one true God. Perhaps, as some claim, Muhammad was just another spoke on the greater spiritual wheel, leading to the same supreme hub Christians and Jews know as God. If so, perhaps a person would be well suited to adopt a more humanitarian posture. So, which spirit is which, or are they the same? Is Allah the same God Christians worship? How can we know for sure? The Bible tells us:

Beloved, do not believe every spirit, but test the spirits,
whether they are of God; because many false prophets
have gone out into the world.

—1 JOHN 4:1

Nor give place to the devil.

—EPHESIANS 4:27

Why did our spiritual hedge, built on "In God We
Trust," break down? How did the Muslim terrorists get
around this spiritual hedge? And why could we not see
them coming? Where is our spiritual perception? Where is
our spiritual power? From whence are we seeking our help?
What do we rely on to repel this invasion of evil? Are military and government alliances enough to stop this fury of
absolute evil? What is at the core of the matter? How do
the Qur'an and Bible stack up on these issues? Is Allah only
a masquerade for God Himself, calling for peace with one
side of his forked tongue and for slaughter of them all with
the other? So which side of the equation do you believe,
peace or death? Are they related? Which shell is the truth
under? We will examine the Qur'an, the purported book of
peace, which unobtrusively says:

But when the forbidden months are past, then fight
and slay the pagans wherever ye find them and seize
them, beleaguer them and lie in wait for them in every
stratagem (of war).

—SŪRAH 9:5

Disguised as religious men of peace, imams (scholars)
lead their fellow Muslims with dark, foreboding spirits,
extending their bondage and patiently awaiting an opportunity to strike at unbelievers. Their martyrs press forward on command, demonized, the fulfilled product of

fundamentalist Islam. Like bloodthirsty fiends they linger, slithering forward, hissing ever louder, finally exposing deadly fangs, fangs that have now bitten into the very heart of America. And those responsible, driven by this spirit of terror, rejoice. They have obeyed the dictates of the Qur'an.

> Against them make ready your strength to the utmost of your power, including steeds of war, to strike terror into (the hearts of) the enemies of Allah…Whatever ye spend in the cause of Allah shall be repaid unto you, and ye shall not be treated unjustly.
> —Sürah 8:60

> Let those fight in the cause of Allah who sell the life of this world for the Hereafter, to him who fighteth in the cause of Allah, whether he is slain or gets victory, soon shall We give him a reward of great (value).
> —Sürah 4:74

Muslim warriors (Mujahedeen) give Allah pleasure. "It is not fitting for an Apostle that he should have prisoners of war until he hath thoroughly subdued the land" (Sürah 8:67). How pleased was Allah with the carnage and death at the World Trade Center? How pleased was Allah to receive the souls of the terrorists? Hidden under any guise, malevolent spirits drive such enraged madmen to more terror, driven by promises of sensual immortality like a drug stupor. So the Qur'an so eloquently promises with articulated images the martyr's heaven.

> They are to cohabit with demure virgins…as beauteous as corals and rubies…full-breasted maidens for playmates…in the gardens of delight…They're to lie face to face on jeweled couches, and be serviced by

10

immortal youths…young boys, their personal property, as comely as virgin pearls…We created the *houris* [dancing girls] and made them virgins, carnal playmates for those on the right hand…We are going to wed them to dark-eyed *houris*.

—Sūrah 55:56, 58; 78:33; 56:12; 52:16–17, 24; 56:35–38; 52:20

A powerful and determined army cannot be assembled unless its potential warriors are conscious of a clear distinction between vice and virtue. Realizing this fact, Muhammad devised the plan of *jihad*, based on sex, plunder and world conquest. Carnal gratification, man's greatest desire, is the first temptation *jihad* carries. A Mujahedeen warrior who once suffered pangs of sexual starvation in the torrid sands of Arabia was promised plenty of sensual enjoyment as a reward for participating in carnage, whether or not he survived the rigors of the battlefield. If the Mujahedeen got killed, he was assured that the *houris* (dancing girls) waited for his glorious company in Jannah (paradise), and if he survived, he had a share in the plunder, which also included the women of the infidels. In our vernacular, it was a win-win situation.

Many verses in the Qur'an forbid sexual intercourse outside wedlock. Marriage is a must for the fulfillment of sensual desires, but this law is blown way off course when it comes to the Mujahedeen. During the battle of Autas, the Muslims captured some women along with their husbands. Though earlier a Muslim had been forbidden sexual intercourse with an unbelieving married woman, at this occasion, it was revealed to the Prophet that Allah had relaxed this restriction and permitted intercourse for the warrior if she had fallen to his lot in the battle and thus became his property. The captured men were all murdered.[3]

11

Therefore, when you meet the Unbelievers (in fight), smite at their necks; at length, when ye have thoroughly subdued them, bind a bond firmly (on them)…(He lets you fight) in order to test you, some with others. But those who are slain in the way of Allah, He will never let their deeds be lost.
—SŪRAH 47:4

So, filled with these promises, each believing Muslim man gives a lifetime of obedience in order to be rewarded after death with a specified number of virgins, an unspecified number of pretty boys and seventy-two heavenly *houris* to serve him for eternity.[4]

If the warrior lived, he enjoyed earthly plunder, which often referred to sex as well. A plunderer had to be ruthless with no sympathy for the victim.

But (now) enjoy what ye took in war, lawful and good.
—SŪRAH 8:69

To make his followers merciless looters, Muhammad thoroughly drilled them in hatred of non-Muslims, the potential victims.

For the worst of beasts in the sight of Allah are those who reject Him: They will not believe.
—SŪRAH 8:55

Lo! Allah is an enemy to those who reject faith.
—SŪRAH 2:98

O ye who believe! Fight the Unbelievers who gird you about, and let them find firmness in you.
—SŪRAH 9:123

Fight those who believe not…until they pay the Jizya

with willing submission, and feel themselves subdued.

—SŪRAH 9:23

It simply means that a true Muslim sells himself to Allah in return for paradise; he is a paid soldier whose only aim in life is to kill infidels or get killed. A hadith from Al Bokhari 4, says, "Paradise lies under the shade of swords." Muhammad also said, "Acting as Allah's soldier for one night in a battlefield is superior to saying prayers at home for 1000 years."[5]

Misled Muslims are in deep bondage to dark, demonic spirits that systematically compel them toward furious and unspeakable evil acts. The Muslim people are forced to accept the will of Allah with no alternative. Muslims are not allowed to even consider the love of the Messiah and Savior Jesus Christ. Anyone distributing Bibles is to be immediately killed. If a Muslim converts to Christianity, he too is to be killed. Muslims do not adopt the humanitarian notion of freedom of religion. All nonbelievers are considered oppressors and transgressors because they do not follow the will of Allah as presented in the Qur'an.

> Fighting is prescribed for you, and ye dislike it. But it is possible that ye dislike a thing which is good for you and that ye love a thing which is bad for you. But Allah knoweth, and ye know not.
>
> —SŪRAH 2:216

> And fight them on until there is no more tumult or oppression, and there prevail justice and faith in Allah; but if they cease, let there be no hostility except to those who practice oppression.
>
> —SŪRAH 2:193

> Fight in the cause of Allah those who fight you, but do

not transgress limits, for Allah loveth not transgressors.

—SŪRAH 2:190

The bombing of the World Trade Center marks a turning point in the U.S. confrontation with terrorism. Previously, American citizens overseas had been targeted, leaving U.S. territory virtually unscathed, until now. Should festering tensions escalate, nuclear war could ensue. Islamic nations, with fundamentalist sentiments running rampant in the streets, have about three dozen nuclear weapons, highly enriched with uranium. Should those components fall into the hands of radical fundamentalist terrorists, the results could be catastrophic. Humanity needs God and His love before it's too late. Nineteen fundamentalist terrorist martyrs crashed their hijacked planes into the World Trade Center and the Pentagon, and nineteen died. They killed over five thousand innocent people. And those responsible rejoice and invoke the following eerie verse.

> O Apostle! Rouse the Believers to the fight. If there are twenty amongst you, patient and persevering, they will vanquish two hundred: if a hundred, they will vanquish a thousand of the Unbelievers: for these are a people without understanding.
> —SŪRAH 8:65

> And slay them wherever ye catch them, and turn them out from where they have turned you out; for tumult and oppression are worse than slaughter.
> —SŪRAH 2:191

> For the Unbelievers are unto you open enemies.
> —SŪRAH 4:101

Seize them and slay them wherever ye find them; and (in any case) take no friends or helpers from their ranks.

—SÜRAH 4:89

Remember thy Lord inspired the angels (with the message): I am with you: give firmness to the Believers: I will instill terror into the hearts of the Unbelievers: smite ye above their necks and smite all their finger-tips off them.

—SÜRAH 8:12

Then fight and slay the pagans wherever ye find them and seize them, beleaguer them and lie in wait for them in every stratagem (of war).

—SÜRAH 9:5

Fight those who do not believe in Allah…until they pay the Jizya [tax] with willing submission, and feel themselves subdued.

—SÜRAH 9:29

Truly Allah loves those who fight in His Cause in battle array, as if they were a solid cemented structure.

—SÜRAH 61:4

They will not fight you (even) together, except in fortified townships, or from behind walls. Strong is their fighting (spirit) amongst themselves: thou wouldst think they are united, but their hearts are divided: that is because they are a people devoid of wisdom.

—SÜRAH 59:14

The free world has had its wake-up call. We have a clear chance to reunite with God. We have the opportunity to heal our land. The Lord God states:

15

> If My people who are called by My name will humble themselves, and pray and seek My face, and turn from their wicked ways, then I will hear from heaven, and will forgive their sin and heal their land.
>
> —2 CHRONICLES 7:14

We have another chance to be under one God, indivisible, with justice for all. We have a chance for real peace. We have a chance to unite our nation in love, to shed titles of black, white, brown, yellow or red. We have a chance to love one another and call ourselves Americans with true freedom and true unity of purpose. But terrorists would disagree and are set on destruction. But we are not to fear terrorists.

> Have I not commanded you? Be strong and of good courage; do not be afraid, nor be dismayed, for the LORD your God is with you wherever you go.
>
> —JOSHUA 1:9

It is sometimes only in the aftermath of a severe tragedy that we again see the landscape of majesty and godliness. We need to put God in front like never before. When the Holy Spirit of God, housed in the ark of the covenant, was carried before King David and the Hebrew army, they were never defeated. They took every bit of land they traversed. This same Holy Spirit is now available to all mankind, to live within us. He is our Comforter, our Teacher, our Power and our Guide for the days to come. We ask and pray that the Holy Spirit fill us with love and courage as we struggle to understand.

> For the Holy Spirit will teach you in that very hour what you ought to say.
>
> —LUKE 12:12

> The Helper, the Holy Spirit, whom the Father will send

16

in My [Jesus] name, He will teach you all things, and
bring to your remembrance all things that I said to you.
—JOHN 14:26

We must reject media stereotypes and listen to the voice
of the Holy Spirit, for God loves all men. We have a stellar
opportunity to help Muslims overcome their bondage.
There are many Arabs who care about a peaceful life, rais-
ing their children and providing for their families. Many
young Arabic men and women dream of coming to
America to enjoy freedoms they don't have in their own
countries. We must find ways to reach them and give them
the true freedom found in Jesus, who said, "The thief does
not come except to steal, and to kill, and to destroy. I have
come that they may have life, and that they many have it
more abundantly" (John 10:10). Jesus even loves bin Laden
and his confederates, and He desires that none of them perish, but come to everlasting life (2 Pet. 3:9).

Jesus died on the cross and gave His life to save all sinners,
and His followers must be willing to lay down their lives to
bring this good news to the world. Biblical salvation is a free
gift paid for by the death of Jesus, who said, "Go into all the
world and preach the gospel to every creature" (Mark 16:15).
Jesus' command includes today's over one billion Muslims,
who present a tremendous and inescapable challenge to
every Christian. The good news must be brought to those
who may be killed for believing it or who may kill us for
offering it. To die fighting unbelievers is the only sure way
for a Muslim to gain paradise. Yet Christ also died for
Muslims, and His love compels us.

Muslims are quick to claim we worship the same God.
But the Jesus in the Qur'an is not the Jesus of the Bible.
The Jesus in the Bible is God the Son who died on the
cross for our sins. The Jesus in the Qur'an is not God the
Son, and He did not die on the cross for our sins. Hence,

the denial of Jesus as God the Son spotlights an antichrist.

> O People of the Book! Commit no excesses in your religion: nor say of Allah aught but truth. Christ Jesus the son of Mary was (no more than) an Apostle of Allah...Say not "Trinity": desist: it will be better for you: for Allah is One God: Glory be to Him: (for Exalted is He) above having a son.
>
> —SŪRAH 4:171

> In blasphemy indeed are those that say that God is Christ the son of Mary.
>
> —SŪRAH 5:17

> O ye who believe! Take not the Jews and the Christians for your friends and protectors: they are but friends and protectors to each other. And he amongst you that turns to them (for friendship) is of them.
>
> —SŪRAH 5:51

> They do blaspheme who say: "God is Christ the son of Mary."... They do blaspheme who say: God is one of three in a Trinity: for there is no God except one God Allah. If they do not desist from their word (of blasphemy), verily a grievous penalty will befall the blasphemers among them...Christ the son of Mary was no more than a Apostle; many were the Apostles that passed away before him.
>
> —SŪRAH 5:72–73, 75

Some Westerners naively accept Allah, who inspired Muhammad, as the God of the Bible. Yet Allah has no son. In spite of the place accorded Jesus in the Qur'an, the Jesus of Islam is not the Jesus of the Bible, but another Jesus.

There are some who trouble you and want to pervert

18

the gospel of Christ. But even if we, or an angel from heaven, preach any other gospel to you than what we have preached to you, let him be accursed.

—GALATIANS 1:7-8

Christianity and its message of salvation through Jesus Christ the Son of God are under attack. The definition of an antichrist is one that denies Jesus as the Son of God and denies that there is salvation in Him. If Christians are to survive and drive back this dark evil, we must lift up Jesus in this hour of peril through prayer, worship, understanding and love. If we lift Jesus up, He will draw Muslims as well as all mankind to Himself. When they find Jesus, they too will have the peace that surpasses all understanding, joy unspeakable and His eternal love.

And I [Jesus], if I am lifted up from the earth, will draw all peoples to Myself.

—JOHN 12:32

2

Muhammad, the Connection

> But evil men and impostors will grow worse and
> worse, deceiving and being deceived.
> —2 Timothy 3:13

Muhammad is the sole founder and key personality in the advent and subsequent rise of Islam. He is often portrayed nobly poised on a black steed set against a backdrop of shifting, wind-swept sands. His medium, lean frame, dark, thick beard and deeply weathered face frame mysterious piercing eyes set in a large head eccentrically poised on massive shoulders. It has been noted that from under his black desert shroud his eyes have penetrated into the hearts of those around him. This image, taken from the supplemental Islamic writings, has created the "Arabian Nights" mystique of Muhammad in the West. His coffin is said to hang forever in midair "between heaven and earth," like the bodies of ancient sacred kings.

Muhammad was an eloquent preacher, a spiritual mystic who fully surrendered to the bidding of a sinister spiritual reality. Today, the belief systems that he instituted stretch forth like the unrelenting sands of the Sahara Desert, consuming mankind and darkening souls as it spreads. His commands still bind, kill and terrorize innocent people, and more than a thousand years after he first uttered *jihad*, blood continues to flow.

It is claimed by some Muslims that the mission of their prophet Muhammad was to establish a new religion with a new code of law that would replace the corrupt and outdated religious system of the Jews and the Christians. For this reason, many Muslims sense no need to give any attention to the message of Christianity. To them, the Christian religion has been superseded by a new and better religion, the religion Islam, introduced by Muhammad to the world almost six hundred years after the time of Christ. Though this thinking has spread into much of Islam, it is not in line with the teaching of the Qur'an.

His followers called Muhammad the Commander of the Faithful, the Lawgiver and the Prophet with the Sword. Though he first suffered mild persecution, Muhammad used diplomacy and persistence to engulf the loosely knit idolaters of Mecca. He started his campaign in the ancient fertility religion that worshiped the moon god, which was always the dominant religion of Arabia. The moon god was worshiped by praying toward Mecca several times a day, making an annual pilgrimage to the Kabah, which was a temple of the moon god, running around the Kabah seven times, caressing an idol of a black stone set in the wall of the Kabah, running between two hills, making animal sacrifices, gathering on Fridays for prayers and giving alms to the poor. Though now incorporated into Islam, these pagan rites were practiced by the idol-worshiping Arabs long before Muhammad was born. This explains why the

21

crescent moon is the symbol of Islam. Every time you see the Islamic symbol of a crescent moon, you are seeing the ancient symbol of the moon god.

Due to various means of coercion, most of the surrounding idolaters eventually threw in with Muhammad. Once he had this base from which to operate, tremendous growth followed. His growing hordes gorged on easy spoil and sexual conquest. For the leadership of the poor disjointed idolaters, he was a godsend, for they too shared in the spoils of war. Muhammad was tactical in his dealings with his conquered foes. He would craftily pardon the opposition when victory was certain and thus gain loyal support for sparing their lives. Through ensuing wars, Arabia, as the Middle East was then called, became vulnerable and was overwhelmed within a century.

Muhammad had not initially been given permission to fight or shed blood, but he was ill treated and accused of lying. Frustrated, he found permission from Allah to fight and to protect himself against those who wronged his followers and treated them badly. As his influence grew, Muhammad began to claim he was the confirmation and climax of all prophets, of which no more were to come. He expected Jews and Christians to recognize him as a continuation and final word of their Scriptures. When they pointed out his perversions and obvious misunderstandings, he was at first disappointed, then extremely vindictive. They labeled him a heretic and a madman. This totally enraged Muhammad, and he began a zealous and murderous quest to subdue them. His inspirations ran rampant, and he formulated the concept of *jihad*.

D. L. Moody once said, "The world has yet to see what God can do with one surrendered soul." A surrendered vessel is capable of great things, and God seeks such that would serve Him. We need only study the great prophets of old and what they were able to accomplish with full surrender to God. But this principle holds equally true for anyone doing Satan's bidding. Satan can only work when he is given fertile ground and a willing heart in which to operate, and his spirits search for willing vehicles, too. Muhammad was such a medium.

Muhammad was born in the stony valley of Mecca around A.D. 570 in the Quarish tribe, which dominated the area. Mecca was then a well-watered layover on the early spice and incense road. It was a lawless time as the idolatrous civilization was breaking down and Europe had plunged into the Dark Ages. There were many wars nearby amid general economic chaos.

Muhammad's father was named Abd Allah. He died before Muhammad was born. His mother's name was Anima, and she died before he was six. A woman named Halima nursed Muhammad when he was an infant and told his mother that she thought he was possessed. Halima returned Muhammad to her many times. When he was five years old, he became uncontrollable, and she would take him no more. Muhammad, meaning the "praised one," was so named by his grandfather Abd al-Muttalib, who had now taken him. His grandfather was said to have been a custodian for the Kabah. But he died two years later, and Muhammad then went to live with his paternal uncle.

Muhammad spent his young life as an orphaned and, as history arguably has it, illiterate camel driver. During his youth he tended sheep and goats on the hillsides surrounding Mecca. As he grew older he began to make frequent trips between Mecca and Syria with his uncle. He is said to have been a fast walker, a handsome youth and to have grown to be an impressive and somewhat charismatic character. The emphasis of charity to orphans in the Qur'an is easily attributable to his early life as an orphan.

When Muhammad was twenty-five years old and residing in Mecca, his uncle persuaded him to work as a caravan manager for Khadija, the daughter of Khuwailid. She was a rich widow with a Christian background. One day he received a message from her in which she fondly elucidated his better characteristics. The message ended with a marriage proposal. They eventually married, and she became his first convert. They had four daughters, and her wealth gave him the leisure and opportunity to contemplate the destiny of his fellow men. Fired by his own vision and the support of Khadija, he set out to change the face of Arabia. She was fifteen years older than Muhammad, and died at the age of sixty-five.

After Khadija's death, Muhammad married at least fifteen other women and had numerous concubines. Most of his brides were in their teens, the youngest of which was a ten-year-old named Ayisha. One of his wives said that he had a passion for young women, scents and that he liked to eat. He forbade any of his wives from marrying after his death.

One of Muhammad's first converts was his adopted son Zeyd Ibn Aretha, who divorced his wife—and then Muhammad married her. This caused a great upheaval and scandal among Muhammad's followers. When he was asked why he could marry her, he promptly had another revelation. He changed the social custom by decree and made up convenient new verses for the Qur'an.

> Allah gave her to you in marriage, so that it should become legitimate for true believers to use the wives of their adopted sons if they divorced them. Allah's will needs be done. No blame shall be attached to the prophet for doing what is sanctioned for him by Allah.
> —Sūrah 33:37

> O Prophet! We have made lawful to thee thy wives to whom thou hast paid their dowers; and those whom thy right hand possesses out of the prisoners of war

whom Allah has assigned to thee; and daughters of thy paternal uncles and aunts, and daughters of thy maternal uncles and aunts...this only for thee, and not for the Believers (at large).

—SŪRAH 33:50

Muhammad also took one-fifth of all the booty that was recovered during battles with infidels. The rest he gave to his soldiers to keep them rampaging. Soon thereafter, the Qur'an officially proclaimed that one-fifth of all plunder belonged to him. Such messages were coincidentally revealed to Muhammad directly from heaven in order to justify his deeds and conduct. If he had already given a verse and changed his mind, he would annul the first verse.

None of Our revelations do We abrogate or cause to be forgotten, but We substitute something better or similar; knowest thou not that Allah hath power over all things? Knowest thou not that to Allah belongeth the dominion of the heavens and the earth! And besides Him ye have neither patron nor helper.

—SŪRAH 2:106–107

Whenever Muhammad needed divine backing, Allah sanctioned murder, adultery, theft, greed and any other excess his whims desired. It's no mistake that the conquering madman's heaven consisted of booty, alluring virgins, young boys, concubines and sexual pleasures. What began as a weak facade under the guise of revelation and religion has ended up in a religious cataclysm of debauchery and murder.

An entire chapter named Prohibition was written when Muhammad was found with a Coptic slave girl he had promised his wife Hafsa he would not see again. Of course, Muhammad got absolution from Allah concerning the matter. The wives were warned that if they didn't keep quiet and shape up, Muhammad would not be able to protect them from Allah.

Despite his excesses and advantageous theological resources, Muhammad still posed in public as a mere humble servant of Allah with no special power of his own. He made it perfectly clear that he served a higher power and that this power influenced his every action. The Qur'an makes it a special point of emphasis that Muhammad was born of earthly parents with no spiritual intervention. He rose from the early obscurity of an everyday life to spearhead this colossal spiritual movement. Much like other men Satan uses to foster religious perversion, Muhammad exhibited sincerity, dedication and a certain charismatic benevolence to further his absolute purpose.

Muhammad is inseparable from Islam, but some followers still implore his intercession. To nullify Jesus Christ, the Qur'an makes it quite clear that no man can intercede. Muhammad stressed his ordinary status for very good reason. Muslims reject even the word *Muhammadan* because any such hint of worship would parallel Christianity and the worship of Jesus. According to Islamic doctrine, Muhammad worked no miracles; he did not heal the sick or raise the dead. Though he called himself a simple prophet who did only the will of Allah and was subject to death, many miracles were attributed to him. Some were attributed to him posthumously.

Muslim biographies emphasize Muhammad's ethical, humanitarian and rational sides. Characterizing Muhammad as an exemplary Muslim, they write that he left behind the perfect vision as to how one should act. Muslims seek Muhammad's guidance in all aspects of their lives. He was considered their judge, ruler, militaristic commander, preacher, visionary, father, husband, brother, tradesman, statesman, peace negotiator and head of state. His life story is limited in the Qur'an, but it is well supplemented with the

Hadith, a vast collection of hundreds of thousands of sayings and accounts of incidents.

Other authors were not so kind. In *The History of the Crusades,* Henry Treece wrote, "Muhammad's so-called revelations were due to sun-crazed musings of a semiliterate trader lulled into a trance by the swaying of his camel."

In the preface to the Qur'an, J. M. Rodwell wrote, "Muhammad was a great though imperfect character, an earnest though mistaken teacher, who was subject to morbid and fantastic hallucinations, and alternations of excitement and depression, which would win for him, in the eyes of his ignorant countrymen, the credit of being inspired."

Muslims do not worship Muhammad, but they emulate him because he is considered a true follower of Allah. Muhammad himself said, "I have no power to benefit or to harm myself except as Allah wills. If I had knowledge of the unseen I would have acquired much. Allah and evil would not have touched me. I am only a warmer and bearer of good tidings to the people who believe."

All through the Qur'an Muhammad's express purpose is to nullify the deity of Jesus and replace Him with Allah. He stresses his own mortal nature, but on the other hand, he is always described as superior to Jesus. Eschatological writings place Muhammad at the Last Judgment instead of Jesus, but have him heroically refusing to enter until all other believers are in. Despite this obvious effort to depict him as an extraordinary mortal man, any supernatural aspects in Islam originated by Muhammad himself. He has attained the platform of the preexisting divine light in the minds of most Muslims. He claimed to see Allah face to face (Sürah 27). He may have seen some angel of light, but he did not see God. After all, he did so claim to be a mere mortal, and he claimed to follow the Bible. The Bible says, "You cannot see My face; for no man shall see Me, and live" (Exod. 33:20).

27

It was during the night journey (*mi`raj*) on the night of power (*qadr*), that Muhammad claimed to first commune with Allah. On that same night he claimed to have been chosen as Allah's messenger. The Qur'an explicitly states, "Muhammad is only a messenger; messengers have passed away before him" (Sürah 3:144).

These events began when Muhammad was about forty. He would retreat to a cave on Mount Hira, a couple of miles from Mecca, to fast and meditate. While in this cave he claimed to have extraordinary spiritual trances and visions. It was in A.D. 610, in what is now called the celebrated Islamic month of Ramadan.

When he was first bombarded with these supernatural experiences, he was terrorized and feared he was going insane. He would retreat to the arms of his wife Khadija for comfort, and it was said that he often contemplated suicide. One particular suicide attempt was said to have been stopped at the edge of a cliff by the angel Gabriel who appeared on a throne in the sky. From that moment on he never faltered again in his fateful mission.

Muhammad claimed it was also the angel Gabriel who appeared to him in the cave and commanded him to "Recite" three times. Islam teaches that the angel Gabriel is the true Holy Spirit, and that the helper mentioned by Jesus was actually Muhammad. But then in another place, the Qur'an calls the Holy Spirit God's breath. At times it calls the Holy Spirit just divine inspiration. Islam cannot properly explain the Holy Spirit, but rather has invented rambling, unintelligible contradictions.

When Muhammad asked the appearing spirit what he was to recite, it said, "Proclaim! (or read!) in the name of the Lord and Cherisher, Who created—created man, out of a (mere) clot of congealed blood: Proclaim! And thy Lord is Most Bountiful—He Who taught (the use of) the Pen—taught man that which he knew not" (Sürah 96:1–5).

28

Early on in his experience Muhammad was racked with doubts, and the weight was excruciating. But his spiritual labors finally gave birth to a new satanic development, a new administration dictated from the dark spiritual kingdom of Satan.

Muhammad became comfortable and a willing mouthpiece. He became the clay, and Satan was the potter. He claimed to receive revelations for the next twenty years. When questioned about the veracity of his revelations, he simply answered that he could easily differentiate between his personal experience and divine will.

Muhammad said that he had a twofold purpose: He was to bring knowledge of Allah to the idol-worshiping people and to set the record straight concerning the Jews and the Christians. He was to correct them. This twofold attack was Satan's measured response to the Resurrection and the subsequent growth of Christianity.

This response mimicked the teachings of the Jews and Christians, as they heavily influenced Muhammad in his youth, and his Christian wife Khadija. Some of his concubines were also young captured Christians and Jews. His doctrine had the same roots, but he detoured the truth with his eventual subversions. Into the tree of life he grafted corruption, and all who adhere to this branch face eternal death. Muhammad related stories of Noah, Adam, Moses, Joseph, Jesus and other biblical personalities. The accounts vary from vivid accurate portrayals to some that are so scant as to lose their meaning and significance without prior biblical knowledge. The misconceptions contained in Muhammad's oracles, whether misguided or planned, show a completely distorted understanding of the Holy Spirit and Scripture.

Muhammad was also greatly influenced by the idolatrous conceptions of the times. There were beliefs that gods or demigods had sexual relations with earthly women. Muhammad said that Christians believed that Mary had intercourse with Allah and Jesus was conceived. Fables of the Far East are replete with such similar accounts. Given the idolatrous venue of the day, it is easy to see how Muhammad was led to believe such a presumptuous inference. Consequently, Muhammad mistook Allah, Jesus and Mary to be a trinity. On this basis he dubbed the New Testament errant and muddled by men.

Muhammad claimed to be equal to Moses and to Jesus, although he claimed that his message was greater than theirs. He imitated Christianity and Judaism in that he abolished the pagan idols and rooted his own doctrine in the antiquities of the Bible. He called his revelations the straight path and stressed that one should believe him and that what Jesus said was true but obsolete. Muhammad said that his message was to be final. There would be no more prophets.

The Bible also tells us of a straight path and warns of the false gates. One enters the straight path through the proper gate. That gate is Jesus Christ.

> Enter by the narrow gate; for wide is the gate and broad is the way that leads to destruction, and there are many who go in by it. Because narrow is the gate and difficult is the way which leads to life, and there are few who find it. Beware of false prophets, who come to you in sheep's clothing, but inwardly they are ravenous wolves.
> —MATTHEW 7:13–15

> Most assuredly, I say to you, I am the door of the sheep…If anyone enters by Me, he will be saved, and will go in and out and find pasture. The thief does not come except to steal, and to kill, and to destroy. I have come that they may have life, and that they may have it more abundantly.
> —JOHN 10:7–10

Muhammad alludes to the door, but he avoids it. His message takes the soul through a different door. His straight path leads away from the Savior and, consequently, straight to hell. Muhammad's only purpose was to develop this path of deception.

The Qur'an charges, "Allah by His Grace guided the Believers to the truth, concerning that wherein they differed. For Allah guides whom He will to a path that is straight" (Sürah 2:213).

But Jesus said, "I am the way, the truth, and the life. No one comes to the Father except through Me" (John 14:6).

Though Muhammad's tactics were often clever indeed, contemporary writers in Europe described him as mad, crazy and a man with epilepsy. Dante, whose plagiarized imagery unmistakably shows up in the Qur'an along with the borrowed biblical notions, called him a sower of schism and discord in the *Divine Comedy*. Muhammad could have had some medical problem that has been described as epilepsy. There are many stories of Muhammad falling off his camel in raving fits, only to arise with another innovative and sparkling revelation.

Muhammad may have had some physical problems, but he was not a lunatic. Quite the contrary, he was possessed with an extraordinary ability and power, much of which was derived from the spirit world. Satan is not altogether stupid. He has been around since day one and has had the benefit of being in heaven. He can impart much knowledge to the willing participant.

There are many historical indiscretions in the Qur'an. Aside from the flagrant biblical deviations, other demented elements persist that help expose its demonic source. For example, Alexander the Great is given the status of a prophet (Sürah 18:83–100). Any hasty historical analysis will show Alexander the Great as a drunken tyrant, an adulterer and a murderer who died early in life due to gluttonous excess. We must remember Muhammad's ambitions and that Satan is a master at deception and confusion. He does not work without rhyme or reason. Were Alexander a prophet during his lifetime, he was Satan's.

But Muhammad was the prophet of renown in Islam. Muhammad is single-handedly responsible for the connection. He drew the blueprint that detours souls from Jesus Christ. Muhammad died shortly after the death of his only infant son, who was born to his Egyptian concubine Mary the Copt. A vehement fever combined with the effects of a revengeful poisoning took his life on June 8, 632. He was sixty-two. His tomb is close to the great mosque in Medina, and unlike Jesus, his body remains in his tomb.

Muhammad had taken the major part, 75 percent, of the Qur'an from the Bible and perverted it. Muhammad himself added the rest of the verses in the Qur'an. He dangles exposed for all to see the deception he helped foster.

The Bible warns of such treachery: "Every word of God is pure; He is a shield to those who put their trust in Him. Do not add to His words, lest He reprove you, and you be found a liar" (Prov. 30:5–6).

Muhammad's name is never once predicted, or for that matter, even mentioned in the Bible. The coming of the false prophets is.

3

The Master of Terror and Confusion

The thief does not come except to steal, and to kill, and to destroy. I [Jesus] have come that they may have life, and that they may have it more abundantly.

—JOHN 10:10

Children's stories often depict Satan as a sinister, ugly character with horns, long tail and a pitchfork. But that appearance certainly would not gain the number of converts and foster the huge enduring religion he desired. Satan can assume any guise from a religious man of peace to a crazed terrorist. Though the Bible says he was scorched by God's power and is now a reproach, he is also a liar, and he can only exact worship if he convinces people that he is a wonderful god.

Satan is most effective in times of turmoil. He operates best in confusion, of which he is the author. Hitler unified a reeling Germany deep in economic depression. Once firmly in control, he began his murderous crusade for supremacy.

Satan wants to rule, to be God. To do so, he disguises and conceals his real intentions. He cloaks his purpose under banners of righteousness and nurtures it alongside authentic needs of reform and justice. Once firmly in control, his real motives manifest. The diabolic master has coached many a false prophet. Muhammad was simply one of them.

Muhammad began with an honorable effort. He eradicated idol worship and proclaimed one God. He taught benevolence and preached against violence, but ultimately this changed, and Satan used Muhammad to construct a false scripture by which people are thrust into utter darkness and confusion. Jesus warned, "Beware of false prophets, who come to you in sheep's clothing, but inwardly they are ravenous wolves" (Matt. 7:15).

Satan has assumed the name Allah as his own for his Islamic masquerades as the high god. He demands worship only as the Qur'an directs. From this assumed godship he has confused and thrashed the Islamic world. For the sake of this world, this reality must not be confined to whispers. It must be heard! The light of truth must shine on the darkness. When the sun rises, the darkness is dispelled. Jesus is that sun, and Jesus commands all true believers, "You are the light of the world. A city that is set on a hill cannot be hidden. Nor do they light a lamp and put it under a basket, but on a lampstand, and it gives light to all who are in the house" (Matt. 5:14–15).

The Bible forewarned of Satan's treachery: "Woe to the inhabitants of the earth and the sea! For the devil has come down to you, having great wrath, because he knows that he has a short time" (Rev. 12:12).

Satan, the master of terror and confusion, has already made his choice. He made it long ago, and he made it in full knowledge of God. He has developed a scenario by which he exacts worship while he gorges himself on blood. His throne sits at the root of Islam, with the many fallen angels and rulers of the darkness of this age. We pray that many would escape his clutches, whether Islamic or otherwise. The Bible warns, "Be sober, be vigilant; because your adversary the devil walks about like a roaring lion, seeking whom he may devour" (1 Pet. 5:8).

We believe Jesus can protect anyone from this murderer and thief. Jesus said, "And I give them eternal life, and they shall never perish; neither shall anyone snatch them out of My hand" (John 10:28).

When a serial killer, a political madman or an insane person is apprehended, there is little mistake concerning the perpetrated evil. History easily unravels the corrupt and debaucherous mind. But the snake we expose is far cleverer than the common rogue. When murder is committed under the guise of his skillful religious confusion, under the name of a god, the gray enigma of confusion can carry the standards of destruction for centuries. It is written, "Now the serpent was more cunning than any beast of the field which the LORD God had made" (Gen. 3:1).

At one time this evil master, Satan, was the most beautiful of God's creatures. After his fall, he used his knowledge and appeal to beguile Adam and Eve to eat of the forbidden tree of knowledge. As in Islam, he claimed to provide the mind of God, to know God's will. Thus he confused them. He created doubt. He asked them if they had heard God correctly. Then he denied what God really said and interjected a lie. God had clearly said, "Of the tree of the knowledge of good and evil you shall not eat" (Gen. 2:17). Satan said, "For God knows that in the day you eat of it your eyes will be opened, and you will be like God, knowing good and evil" (Gen. 3:5).

Outright lies and distorted half-truths are meshed and veiled in and among the many moral codes and verses of compassion found in the Qur'an. The Bible explains of Satan, "He was a murderer from the beginning, and does not stand in the truth, because there is no truth in him. When he speaks a lie, he speaks from his own resources, for he is a liar and the father of it" (John 8:44).

Lying is Satan's forte. He is quite capable of luring the coyest of minds. Without Jesus and His truth, anyone is vulnerable. Satan will try anything from torture to a grandiose seduction. He may present logic, a humanitarian gesture or, more dangerously, a sublime angelic religion. It is written, "That serpent of old, called the Devil and Satan, who deceives the whole world; he was cast to earth, and his angels were cast out with him" (Rev. 12:9).

Islam conceals a master spider, and the Qur'an is the web. Satan's venom causes eternal death for the soul. It is a most treacherous poison, because it not only kills others, but also its own members. But the Bible admonishes: "And do not fear those who kill the body but cannot kill the soul. But rather fear Him who is able to destroy both body and soul in hell" (Matt. 10:28).

The name *Satan* literally means adversary. It's a Hebrew word found throughout the Bible. He has many other names, such as tempter, prince of the world, god of this age, prince and power of the air, and the accuser of the brethren. He is resourceful and unrelenting (John 8:44; 1 John 3:8; Rev. 12:10; 1 Pet. 5:8). Like other angels, Satan has an intellect, emotions and a will. He is seen as a serpent, a dragon or an angel of light (Rev. 12:9; 2 Cor. 11:14). He is mentioned in seven Old Testament books, and every writer of the New Testament mentions him. Jesus also taught us of Satan (Matt. 12:39; Luke 10:8; 11:18).

The master behind Islam is a spirit, once the highest of all angels (Ezek. 28:14; Eph. 6: 11–12). God created him pure and sinless. God gave him a free will. Exercising that free will, he made his deliberate choice in full knowledge of the infinite goodness and holiness of the Creator. Consequently, his choice is irretrievable. His doom is sealed. He had been privileged in heaven until his fall, but he wanted to be like the Most High God.

> How fallen you are from heaven, O Lucifer, son of the morning! How you are cut to the ground, you who weakened the nations! For you have said in your heart: "I will ascend into heaven, I will exalt my throne above the stars of God: I will sit on the mount of the congregation of the farthest sides of the north; I will ascend above the heights of the clouds, I will be like the Most High."
>
> —Isaiah 14:12–14

Overemphasize the devil? Never! Rather, lift the rock that the snake of terrorism hides under and shine the scorching light of truth directly on him. Every creature of darkness will head for the gutter when truth is shone upon him or her. The Bible has forewarned of the present-day treachery: "In latter times some will depart from the faith, giving heed to deceiving spirits and doctrines of demons, speaking lies and hypocrisy" (1 Tim. 4:1–2).

In heaven Satan was allowed to walk into God's most holy inner sanctum, the holy mountain of fire. He had free reign to do things that were select. It is written of Satan:

> You were the seal of perfection, full of wisdom and perfect in beauty. You were in Eden, the garden of God; every precious stone was your covering: the sardius, topaz, and diamond, beryl, onyx, and jasper, sapphire, turquoise, and emerald with gold. The workmanship of your timbrels and pipes was prepared for you on the day you were created. You were the anointed cherub who covers; I established you; you were on the holy mountain of God; you walked back and forth in the midst of the fiery stones. You were

perfect in your ways from the day you were created, till iniquity was found in you.

—EZEKIEL 28:12–15

The Bible warns us of Satan assuming godship: "Let no one deceive you by any means … the man of sin is revealed, the son of perdition, who opposes and exalts himself above all that is called God or that is worshiped, so that he sits in the temple of God, showing himself that he is God" (2 Thess. 2:3–4).

His was a sin of pride: "Your heart was lifted up because of your beauty; you corrupted your wisdom for the sake of your splendor… You defiled your sanctuaries by the multitude of your iniquities, by the iniquity of your trading; therefore I brought fire from your midst; it devoured you, and I turned you to ashes upon the earth in the sight of all who saw you. All who knew you among the peoples are astonished at you; you have become a horror, and shall be no more forever" (Ezek. 28:17–19).

Jesus gave us a way to deal with the master of terror and confusion. We need not fear Satan and his tactics, and we need not give in to his demands. The Bible tells us, "Resist the devil and he will flee from you" (James 4:7); "He who is in you is greater than he who is in the world" (1 John 4:4); and, "God has not given us the spirit of fear, but of power" (2 Tim. 1:7).

Jesus told His disciples that the enemy would come and sow tares among the good wheat. Endless pains are taken by Satan to sow these tares. He has sown doctrines of deceit since antiquity. We are told that the apostles also had to deal with false doctrine: "For we did not follow cunningly devised fables" (2 Pet. 1:16). The Bible tells us that the tares will be allowed to remain until the harvest time. Then angels will come and separate them from the wheat. The tares will then be thrown into the fire (Matt. 13:24–30).

The master of terror and confusion uses clever and witty stories designed to subtly capture the mind of the hearers. The following is a typical fable as told by the Islamic philosopher Rumi. A man traveled from a faraway land to call on King Solomon. While on his journey the man was visited by the angel of death. He was terrified. Upon arriving at the king's palace, the man, believing that the angel had looked upon him angrily, appealed to the king that he might be whisked away to India by the four winds, which were often said to obey the king's commands.

Solomon deliberated, and then granted the man's request. Then Solomon asked the angel of death concerning the matter. The angel replied, "I did not look upon the man angrily, but in amazement, for Allah had ordered me to kill the man in distant India; seeing him here I wondered, thinking perhaps Allah was mistaken. I have now learned never to doubt Allah's decrees."

Such stories are designed to capture the mind and to get the soul through the doors of Satan's wicked spiritual kingdom. But Jesus says, "Most assuredly, I say to you, he who does not enter the sheepfold by the door, but climbs up some other way, the same is a thief and a robber...Most assuredly, I say to you, I am the door of the sheep...If anyone enters by Me, he will be saved, and go in and out and find pasture" (John 10:1, 7, 9).

It is also written, "[Many] will turn their ears away from the truth, and be turned aside to fables" (2 Tim. 4:4).

Satan controls every basic function of a Muslim's life. The bonds and chains are deep, heavy and intricate. They will only be broken by the power and blood of Jesus Christ. Only Jesus can undo this terror and confusion. "For God is not the author of confusion but of peace" (1 Cor. 14:33).

The Bible tells us that we can expect Satan to lie (Acts 5:3). He will accuse us daily (Rev. 12:10). He will hinder God's work, and he will send demons to attack God's people

(1 Thess. 2:18; Eph. 6:11–12). Satan will present confusion, temptation and immorality, and he will sow tares among the good seed and persecute us (1 Cor. 7:5; Matt. 13:38–39; Rev. 12:10). Satan binds minds, steals God's Word from us and uses men to oppose the work of God (2 Cor. 4:4; Luke 8:12; Rev. 2:13). His forces are gathering for one final attempt at destroying God's people, but the Bible says that he will find his end in the lake of fire (Rev. 20:13; 16:13–14; 19:20).

> The devil, who deceived them, was cast into the lake of fire and brimstone where the beast and the false prophet are. And they will be tormented day and night forever.
>
> —REVELATION 20:10

Satan even tempted Jesus. Then he made his biggest mistake. He crucified the Son of God. This happened because Jesus came into the world as a humble and ordinary person. What Satan now knows is that his days are numbered. "For the devil has come down upon you, having great wrath, because he knows that he has a short time" (Rev. 12:12).

Like a common criminal the master of terror and confusion has a front for his despicable acts. His religion appears to have some merit on the surface, but when one peers behind the thin veneer, only death, destruction and the loss of salvation are apparent. "And no wonder! For Satan himself transforms himself into an angel of light" (2 Cor. 11:14).

Satan has many of his followers pray all day, give alms to the poor, fast, chant, recite scripture and conduct lives bedecked with the aura of would-be saints. He has them ceremoniously bow at prescribed times of the day, lead prayer and keep Qur'anic verses resonant and profusely flowing from the minarets. But the Bible tells us, "In latter times some will depart from the faith, giving heed to deceiving spirits and doctrines of demons" (1 Tim. 4:1).

If the master of terror and confusion had one army, one religion or one distinct method of attack, the contrast might be readily apparent. The array of satanic weaponry in force today can seem bewildering and overwhelming to the human mind. Humanity is caught in a whirlpool of deceiving "-isms" and terror.

On September 11, 2001, within minutes thousands were dead, trapped or maimed. New York was paralyzed and in a state of terror and confusion. Many countries and many people, ordinary people who just want to get on with life and who are not concerned about politics or big issues, will now face a different future. It may be through escalation and instability, military reprisals, more terrorism or world recession, but life will change. If you are a Christian, you may be struggling with this simple question: "What should my response be?"

Seek God's face and pray, particularly for the injured and dying, their families, the support workers and medical staff. Wartime experience in Britain showed time and again that in such situations, people "rise above themselves" and start to work together like never before. This is happening right now at the affected sites. Keep praying that God will bless those efforts and move people to work together. We do well to remember what Jesus said: "Be of good cheer, I have overcome the world" (John 16:33).

The Lord has given us a splendid psalm to help us deal with the master of terror and confusion:

> He who dwells in the secret place of the Most High
> Shall abide under the shadow of the Almighty.
> I will say of the Lord, "He is my refuge and my
>   fortress;
> My God, in Him will I trust."
> Surely He shall deliver you from the snare of the
>   fowler

And from the perilous pestilence.
He shall cover you with His feathers,
And under His wings you shall take refuge;
His truth shall be your shield and buckler.
You shall not be afraid of the terror by night,
Nor of the arrow that flies by day,
Nor of the pestilence that walks in the darkness,
Nor of the destruction that lays waste at noonday.
A thousand may fall at your side,
And ten thousand at your right hand;
But it shall not come near you.
Only with your eyes shall you look,
And see the reward of the wicked.
Because you have made the Lord, who is my refuge,
Even the Most High, your dwelling place,
No evil shall befall you,
Nor shall any plague come near your dwelling;
For He shall give His angels charge over you,
To keep you in all your ways.
In their hands they shall bear you up,
Lest you dash your foot against a stone.
You shall tread upon the lion and the cobra,
The young lion and the serpent you shall trample
    underfoot.

—Psalm 91:1–13

4

Islam's Advent

Then many false prophets will rise up and deceive
many. And because lawlessness will abound, the love
of many will grow cold.

—Matthew 24:11–12

When Muhammad first introduced his so-called
revelations, the majority of the surrounding
inhabitants were idolaters. Among them were
scattered bands of Jews and Christians. But the vast majority clung to idols made by hand. They lived meagerly on
what was left of the old incense trade road and chief cul-
tural centers of North Arabia. Only a trickle of Eastern
exotica flowed through what was once the legendary kingdom of Sheba. The idolaters had become disjointed by
tribal wars, anarchy and a severe economic decline.
Though they initially resisted Muhammad, it did not take
much to convert them.

At first, the Quarish tribe (descendants of Ishmael)
yearned to slay Muhammad for economic reasons. Being
forewarned, he fled with Abu Bakr, an early convert and

influential merchant, to a cave close to Mecca. Abu Bakr was Muhammad's close friend throughout the early days and was instrumental in the early success of Islam. Osama bin Laden feels very close to Muhammad as he hides in caves. After the fourth day of their hiding, they fled to Yathrib (present-day Medina, which is 320 miles from Mecca). It was June 25, A.D. 622. This flight marks the first day in the Muslim calendar and is called "The *Hijra*" (the journey).[1]

Muhammad's expanding hordes fervently sought the blessings and spoils that Allah promised they could keep through conquest. From the sultry oasis of Medina, with what could only be described as poor Bedouins from the sand and lava wastes of Arabia, Islam arose and subdued a considerable part of the world.

The Islamic kingdom eventually stretched from Gibraltar to the Himalayas and was only halted at the gates of Vienna. The Christian counterattacks that followed were the infamous crusades. Much of the aggression that followed in waves of successive assaults was a gross overreaction. It is a black mark on what tried to pass as Christianity. The crusaders attempted to achieve the kingdom of God on earth by worldly methods.

The newly conquered empires of Persia, Mesopotamia, Syria, Egypt and North Africa were required to pay tribute money to Muhammad. The converted Muslims, those who had recently been desert nomads, moved to lavish garrisons and surrounded themselves with the newly acquired wealth, armies, slaves and concubines. It was an extravagant lifestyle unknown by their ancestors. Muhammad stressed that this plunder was the blessings of Allah. Many more followed and became greedy for Islam.

Before Islam's advent and expansion, Satan's grip in this area had begun to slip. Muhammad's purpose had been challenged by the profuse spread of Christianity. Jesus' doctrine of love had begun to convert the idol worshipers.

The Qur'an was Satan's answer, an adjustment he originated to thwart and distort the authentic Scripture and its message of salvation in Jesus Christ.

Muhammad picked Allah to be the one true God. The name *Allah* originally came from an idol named Alilah. Alilah was one of three hundred sixty gods originally found in a little stone temple at what is now the famous Kabah shrine. This god was thought of as the creator and had assumed a position of a supreme stone god among the many stone gods. Alilah was the paramount divinity of pagan Arabia. Ninety-nine names or attributes were initially ascribed this stone god. Muhammad added compassionate and merciful.

Alilah literally means the "high god" in Arabic, but in its Sanskrit origins it means "mother" or "goddess." There are many chants and praises written to this stone god. They are found in the ancient Sanskrit writings called *Allopanishad* and *Alladistotra*. But Muhammad stressed that this god was a male and made it a decree. Not to be overlooked is the fact that Muhammad's father's name had been Abd-Allah, meaning "the slave of god."

Nonetheless, Allah has come to mean God to the Arab people. They consider Allah the same God that the Christians and Jews worship. Webster's and Random House dictionaries concur that Allah means the "supreme being" in Arabic and call the name akin to the Hebrew Eloah.

Muhammad ordered the rest of the idols destroyed. He exposed the error of planet worship, especially worship of the local favorite moon. But today the crescent moon and the star emblem of the ancient Semites survive as a symbol of Islam and appears on the flag of many Muslim nations.[2]

No matter how the Qur'an distorts Scripture, a Muslim prays to Allah as God. Allah is now synonymous with the God of Abraham, Isaac and Jacob. We do not dispute Allah as a name for God, but we view the Qur'an as a direct lie from Satan. In the truest sense, the fundamentalist Muslim should be considered a Qur'anist. The salvation of the true God never reaches the Muslim people because they are bound by the perversions written in the Qur'an.

Islam was initially successful because it was simple and straightforward. It was easily communicated to the common folks. In the midst of the multifaceted idolatry, the ever-changing heathen rituals and the blood sacrifices, this new twist had the simple and familiar thread of one God. This was acceptable to a people that had worshiped everything from emperors to animals to stones. But under the guise of this god lie the beast and his all too familiar doctrine of demons.

5

Qur'an, the Blueprint

For I testify to everyone who hears the words of the prophecy of this book: If anyone adds to these things, God will add to him the plagues that are written in this book; and if anyone takes away from the words of the book of this prophecy, God shall take away his part from the Book of Life, from the holy city, and from the things which are written in this book.

—REVELATION 22:18–19

The Qur'an, the book of Islam, is not only the testimony of a false prophet; it is the testimony of an antichrist. It's one of the most stubborn enemies of civilization, liberty and truth that the world has yet known. Yet, so many hearing that testimony today are willing to believe it, to take it to heart, to stand on it and even to die for it, as if it were written by the Spirit of Truth. It's a book that has influenced almost as many people as the Bible and has contributed to the shaping of world history. And it's a book that will greatly influence the events of these last days.

There are scientific errors in the Qur'an. Even Arabian

legends are recounted as actual happenings. The Qur'an contains much superstition and occultism, especially its references to *jinn* (genies). There are also subtle deceptions and absurdities, but the Qur'an's contradictions of the Bible are excused by claiming that the Bible was corrupted. Muhammad said the Qur'an was sent to stand as a guardian over the Bible (Sürah 5:48).

Muslims contend that the Qur'an came to replace the holy books of the Jews and Christians, as contained in the Bible, because they became corrupted, altered, outdated and lost. However, the Qur'an itself says no such thing. Instead, the Qur'an declares that it was sent to confirm the previous revelations. It should be understood that if something is to be confirmed, then that something is of extreme importance, especially if God does the confirming! Notice now the following. The Qur'an did not come to correct, replace, annul, modify or do away with; it came to confirm. Also, Muslims attempt to discredit the validity of the Bible because there is not a single verse in it that mentions Muhammad. There is no hard evidence for the existence of the Qur'an in any form before the last decade of the seventh century, except for the idol that advantageously became Allah.

The Qur'an is more antagonistic to the Christian and Jewish faiths than Communism ever was. In Communist China today, Christianity still thrives. But preaching Christianity in Muslim countries, or confession of Christ by a Muslim, is regarded as high treason—both punishable by death.

When the Qur'an is examined in relation to Muhammad's life, an easy parallel is found to the direction the Qur'an takes and his blend of so-called heavenly inspirations. The Qur'an was heavily influenced by a scant knowledge of Christianity and Judaism, by the day-to-day factors of personal experience, associates and the lustful and murderous preferences of Muhammad's appetites.

God has given mankind a road map to salvation in the form of His written Word. Within His Word abides the answer to eternal life. Muhammad called these revelations incomplete and offered another rendition of the Bible. When the import of the Qur'an and its direction is understood, a clear picture emerges. It easily explains the cause of the terrorism and violence we see increasing in our world today. The seeds to the terrorist mentality are found on its pages.

The media has brought the methods of the Qur'an into our living rooms. Its cameras and commentaries present the indiscriminate violence, confusion and bloodshed, but sadly fail to recognize its heart. Innocent people are being murdered on the basis of a religion that encourages the murder of all that do not believe in its creeds. It encourages terrorism and teaches that suicide squads attain immediate salvation.

Newspapers, daily television accounts and even governments often make the mistake of classifying the terrorist as an aberration, a minority, someone out of the norm. They are viewed as criminals and unlawful agents. But the Qur'an depicts these same people as martyrs and saintly purifiers, upholders of the faith. In fundamentalist Islamic circles, Osama bin Laden is a saint. Such men are described in the Qur'an as shining heralds, as Allah's finest warriors. They are seen as holy warriors that battle the infidels of the great Satan, the idolatrous Christians and the devilish dogs Israel.

Can common ground be found for fruitful discussion between a Christian and Muslim? Is there any hope of reconciliation or moderation in the pages of the Qur'an? Does it profess love? Can we expect compassion or even compromise? What are its roots?

It must be clearly understood that the Qur'an is not a book about religion, but we find a religion in a book. Upon close scrutiny this book declares terrorism as its norm. The West usually views warfare as a last resort. The Qur'an portrays *jihad* as its main fare and killing the highest standard. There are positive truths and godly attributes interspersed within the Qur'an, but its ultimate goal is the death of all who don't follow its way. It is strict, dogmatic and uncompromising. The Bible warns, "There is a way that seems right to a man, but its end is the way of death" (Prov. 14:12).

The major difference between the Bible and the Qur'an is the doctrine of the Incarnation. The entire balance and conflict lie in the divinity of Jesus Christ. The Qur'an vehemently denies that Jesus is God. For the Muslim there is salvation only in the dictates of the Qur'an. But the Bible teaches, "There is no other name [only Jesus] under heaven given among men by which we must be saved" (Acts 4:12).

The Qur'an makes the exact opposite assertion, and thereby becomes suspect. It is in direct opposition to the Bible. In 2 Corinthians 2:11, the Bible tells us that Satan's works do abound, and that we are not to be ignorant of his devices.

The poisonous doctrine that the Qur'an contains affects the very soul and spirit of mankind. Its counterfeit doctrine wreaks havoc and is a scourge on the earth today. It abolishes the real Lord. In God's place, fundamentalist Islam forces mankind to obey a diabolic counterfeit that has assumed godship. These authoritative rules lead the Muslim in all things.

In Christianity, the Holy Spirit is God, the Father is God and Jesus is God. How can that be? They are three manifestations of one God (1 John 5:7). The Spirit of God is needed to understand. The Bible tells us that Scripture is of no private interpretation, but understood when guided by the Holy Spirit. Scripture can be read all day, but without the guidance of the Holy Spirit, it will not be understood. The Bible is written to be understood with the mind of a child, but also to confound the wise. (See 1 Corinthians 1:18–31.)

And it is the Spirit that bears witness, because the Spirit is truth. For there are three that bear witness in heaven: the Father, the Word [Jesus], and the Holy Spirit; and these three are one.

—1 JOHN 5:6–7

And yet, the Qur'an still reads, "This Qur'an is not such as can be produced by other than Allah; on the contrary it is a confirmation of (revelations) that went before it, and a fuller explanation of the Book—wherein there is no doubt—from the Lord of the Worlds" (Sürah 10:37).

But the Bible says, "God is Spirit, and those who worship Him must worship in spirit and in truth" (John 4:24).

By claiming to be absolute and the final word, and by the removal of the Holy Spirit, Satan causes confusion and fosters terrorism. Satan's work of death flourishes in such an incomplete and barren atmosphere. Since both the Bible and the Qur'an claim the absolute truth, one is a lie, for their doctrines are opposed to one another. They have two different plans of salvation and two different lords.

Jesus said, "However, when He, the Spirit of truth, has come, He will guide you into all truth; for He will not speak on His own authority, but whatever He hears He will speak; and He will tell you things to come. He will glorify Me, for He will take of what is Mine and declare it to you" (John 16:13–14).

The Qur'anic plan of salvation admonishes, instructs and warns, but it leaves a person alone and helpless. It compels a person to save himself by fasting, prayer, alms giving, killing and following the myriad of other prescribed behaviors in the Qur'an. One can even strap dynamite to his body and speed up the process by blowing up nonbelievers in the course of *jihad*. Such a person is guaranteed immediate entrance into the Qur'an's kingdom. But mankind is incapable of atoning for sin. The Bible teaches us that we cannot save ourselves and that works cannot save us. "For by grace you have been saved through faith, and that not of yourselves; it is a gift of God, not of works, lest anyone should boast" (Eph. 2:8–9).

The Qur'an states that Allah leads and misleads as he will. (See Sürah 6:125.) Jesus never misleads. He leads in paths of righteousness (Ps. 23:3). Jesus also said, "I will never leave you nor forsake you" (Heb. 13:5).

But the god in the Qur'an will destroy and forsake all who give ear to its lies. Let's look at the logistics of this book. The Qur'an comes from the word *quaraa* and means recitation. Its excerpts are said to be part of an eternally existing book that is said to contain Allah's very own speech. Its verses were said to be delivered by the angel Gabriel from the special eternal book kept in heaven. Certain verses were said to have been bestowed upon the prophets from time to time. According to the Qur'an, Adam, Moses, Noah and Jesus were all to have received its revelations. Muhammad said that these revelations did not exhaust the book, but that adequate disclosures were made for man's needs till the end of time.

The Qur'an is about the size of the New Testament with 77,639 words. It has one hundred fourteen chapters (sürahs), and just over six thousand verses are to be believed by faith. It is the earliest known work of Arabic prose. Each chapter has a brief title and varies in length from three lines to two hundred eighty-six lines that mostly end in jingling rhymes. They follow no chronological order and are arranged with the longest first and the shortest last. A strict chronological order is futile, and some say it is better read from the back to the front.

Whether Muhammad himself could read or write is hotly debated. It is said that the words were inscribed directly on his heart by the angel Gabriel. Abu Bakr, the first caliph and first successor to Muhammad's earthly authority, inscribed or carved verses on walls, palm leaves, sheep bones, shoulder blades of other animals, rocks, leather or whatever else was available. Some were committed to memory. Abu Bakr subsequently combined them and gave them the name *Qur'an*. Zeyd Ibn Habit, one of Muhammad's secretaries, finally put together the official version somewhere between A.D. 644–656. At that time all others were destroyed.

Arabic scholars finalized the Qur'an about twenty years after Muhammad's death in the mid-650s. When Muhammad died there was to be no more revelation expected. There are some secondary sources of Islamic theology, but they are not considered divine in origin. They are accepted on the basis of reasoning by analogy and closely parallel the Qur'an. The Qur'an claims an absolute nature. "It is a book in which all things are written" (Sürah 50:4).

The Qur'an claims to contain the word of God, but refuses to accept Jesus as God. The Bible tells us a very different story. "In the beginning was the Word, and the Word was with God, and the Word was God…And the Word became flesh and dwelt among us, and we beheld His glory" (John 1:1, 14).

The Qur'an claims authority from the Supreme Being, the Creator, God Himself. The god that forged its pages calls himself everlasting, says he doesn't sleep and that he owns everything on heaven and on earth. He says that no one can overcome him, that he is all-high and all-glorious. He claims to be benevolent to those who follow him and lays abomination on those that don't (Sürah 2:255–256; 32:7; 6:125). Allah says that he is seen in the powers of nature and that one must accept him under penalty of death.

But the Bible tells us that Jesus is the Creator and the possessor of all things.

He [Jesus] is the image of the invisible God, the firstborn over all creation. For by Him all things were created that are in heaven and that are on earth, visible
and invisible, whether thrones or dominions or principalities or powers. All things were created through
Him and for Him. And He is before all things, and in
Him all things consist.

—COLOSSIANS 1:15–17

The Muslim views the Qur'an as a Christian views Jesus.
It alone is to be followed as the sole savior. Muhammad is
to the Qur'an as the apostles are to Jesus. A Muslim must
abandon himself to Allah by way of the Qur'an, which
always begins with: "Allah the merciful, the compassionate…" (See Sürah 1.) Muslims are also to begin every activity with this phrase. But the Bible tells us to do everything
in the name of Jesus. "Whatever you do in word or deed,
do all in the name of the Lord Jesus" (Col. 3:17).

Total allegiance must be given to the Qur'an. An overt
reverence is shown to the book. It must be presented in the
most beautiful form possible. No other book may be placed
on it. It must be held above the waist, and all who listen to
it must remain silent. It must never touch the floor, and
believers must wash to purify themselves before touching
it. There is no smoking, eating or drinking allowed while
the book is open or being read. The Qur'an is carried to
war, and verses are worn as amulets or written on banners
and walls. And above all, no one may question its contents.

The highest act of piety for a Muslim is to memorize
its contents. Such a person is called a *hafiz* (protector).
Every *hafiz* recites the Qur'an during the month of
Ramadan. They need not understand what they read, but
must pronounce the words correctly. During this month
the Qur'an can be heard during all hours as it emanates
from the heights of the minarets. It is also considered

meritorious to write out the book.

In the strictest sense, the Qur'an is not to be translated into any other languages. It is not considered an Islamic Bible, but like the Bible, nothing is to be added to it nor is anything to be taken away. Muhammad claimed that it was given to the End-Time rulers, the Arabs, and that it would lose its meaning and become perverted if given to the infidels. It is considered to be sublime and claims to be full of wisdom (Sürah 43:2). Ideally, converts should learn the Arabic language in which it was first given. In this way Muhammad thought to keep it from compromise.

Christianity and Judaism are used as a base for the Qur'an, but a new course is set. Muhammad borrowed the biblical accounts, but his versions differ, some slightly and some grossly misinterpreted. But whoever questions the Qur'an is called an unbeliever, transgressor, oppressor or a wicked one. Such are names given to Christians. The Qur'an claims it has been given to straighten Christians out. It claims to have annulled their mistaken religion.

The Qur'an maintains of itself: "It is not a tale invented, but a confirmation of what went before it—a detailed exposition of all things, and a Guide and a Mercy to any such as believe" (Sürah 12:111). Newborn babes get the call to prayer whispered first in their right ear, then in their left ear. This symbolizes the fact that the newborn was never unaware of Allah. At the age of four all Muslim children must begin to memorize verses. They learn that there is no God but Allah, and they learn to pray to him, prayer that they are told leads to success.

The first chapter is instilled into children. It reads, "In the name of Allah, the compassionate, the merciful. Praise be to Allah, lord of creation, the compassionate, the merciful, king of judgment day. You alone we worship, and to you alone we pray for help. Guide us to the straight path of those you have favored. Not of those who have incurred your wrath, not those who have gone astray" (Sürah 1).

Not only did Muhammad grossly distort and rearrange the Bible, but he also added his own accounts, which he said were new revelations. He did not reveal anything fresh as far as a biblical perspective is concerned, nor did he in any way enhance it. Islam claims parts of the Old Testament, especially the Adamic story, so they claim to have the oldest religion, not the youngest. But errors too numerous concerning Abraham, Moses, the Holy Spirit and Jesus abound in the Qur'an.

Carlyle said of the Qur'an: "A wearisome confused jumble, crude, endless iterations, long-windedness, entanglement, insupportable stupidity in short! Nothing but a sense of duty would carry any European through the Qur'an."

Though most Westerners are far removed from this intense theology and its uncompromising lifestyles, it has come to seriously affect them. This book, which claims to punctuate the one true religion, includes the religious, social, economic, civil, military and legal codes for nearly one-fourth of the world's population. Its ways may be obscure to us, but it affects everyone both directly and indirectly.

Often, when Satan issues forth his confusion, it is not always apparent on the surface. It is frequently accomplished under a shroud of piety, with certain standards of merit. What better guise than to be considered righteous while one kills and plunders with his home filled with wives and concubines to please him on his return? What better way than to have a cozy, virtuous umbrella under which to do the dastardly works? From the pages of this revered blueprint and pious fabrication stretches the satanic hand of death.

We find in the Qur'an a different name that claims to be supreme. This name claims to be the only name given to men by which they may be saved. To be a Muslim the name of Allah must reign supreme. But the Bible says:

> Therefore God also has highly exalted Him [Jesus] and given Him the name which is above every name, that at the name of Jesus every knee should bow, of those in heaven, and of those on earth, and of those under the earth.
>
> —PHILIPPIANS 2:9–10

The rejection of Jesus as the Savior is paramount in the Qur'an. This is the work of an antichrist. It is written, "Little children, it is the last hour; and as you have heard that the Antichrist is coming, even now many antichrists have come, by which we know it is the last hour" (1 John 2:18).

Curiously enough, the Qur'an accepts Satan as an entity. Allah is said to have placed Shatyan, as he is called, among the prophets to test the people as to their worthiness. The Qur'an teaches that it was Satan and not God who tested Abraham when he was to sacrifice his son.

The Qur'an declares, "Never did We send an apostle or a prophet before thee, but, when he framed a desire, Satan threw some (vanity) into his desire: but Allah will cancel anything (vain) that Satan throws in, and Allah will confirm (and establish) His Signs: for Allah is full of knowledge and wisdom" (Sürah 22:52).

A story has it that there was once an Arab who asked Muhammad whether he should tether his camel or put his trust in Allah. Muhammad replied that the man should put his trust in Allah and tether his camel. Satan is not stupid or without experience of human nature. We can rest assured that his battle plans will be highly succinct and his blueprint expertly compiled. He has plied his evil trade since time immemorial. He wants and has always wanted to be worshiped as God. It was the reason he was discharged from heaven. He has managed to deliver a gross counterfeit to mankind. It has taken root and is growing.

Satan has legions of spirits working to insure the continued terrorism and death the Qur'an fosters. Anyone who builds his or her house on the Qur'an will be washed away. It is an evil deception. The house built on the Rock will not fall. Jesus is that Rock. Only He possesses the keys to heaven.

The Bible tells us, "And this is the testimony: that God has given us eternal life, and this life is in His Son. He who has the Son [Jesus] has life; he who does not have the Son of God does not have life" (1 John 5:11–12).

6

The Question of Which Angel

But even if we, or an angel from heaven, preach any other gospel to you than what we have preached to you, let him be accursed.

—GALATIANS 1:8

The spirit who claims to have inspired Muhammad cannot be the Father of our Lord Jesus Christ. Instead he is a spirit full of lies, which took upon itself the old Arabic god Allah, wearing it over his face like a mask and claiming to be God, although he is not God. The spirit of Allah in Islam is an unclean spirit of Satan, who rules with great power in a religious disguise to this very day.[1] (See John 8:30–48.)

Angels are spiritual beings created by Jesus. "For by Him [Jesus] all things were created that are in heaven and that are on earth, visible and invisible, whether thrones or dominions or principalities or powers. All things were created through Him and for Him. And He is before all

JESUS VS. JIHAD

things, and in Him all things consist" (Col. 1:16–17).

Angels are powerful spirits that do the Lord's bidding (Ps. 103:20; 2 Pet. 2:11; 2 Thess. 1:7). They can assume a human form and come to earth. They come to intercede and help us. The Bible tells us, "Some have unwittingly entertained angels" (Heb. 13:2).

Jesus taught of angels (Matt. 18:10). They are described in the Bible as sons of the mighty, sons of God, angels, holy ones, morning stars and princes; they are also called highly intelligent (Ps. 89:6; 8:5; Job 1:6; 2:1; 38:7; Dan. 10:13; Rev. 17:1; 2 Sam.14:20). They do not marry or reproduce, nor do they increase in number (Matt. 13:2). The word *angel* is used two hundred seventy-five times in the Bible and is found in thirty-four of its books.

Angels have different duties that they perform for the Lord. They discharge acts of mercy and take part in spiritual battle. It was the messenger angel Gabriel that Muhammad claimed came to him that fateful day in the cave. He claimed that Allah sent Gabriel to him to set all records straight. As Muhammad claimed, some angels are sent on missions to instruct.

God used Gabriel as a messenger in the Bible. Gabriel will also accompany Jesus at the Second Coming (1 Thess. 4:16). Gabriel once appeared before the prophet Daniel in the form of a man to help interpret a vision. Daniel talked with him and saw him fly swiftly (Dan. 8:16; 9:21). The angel Gabriel also came directly from the presence of God to bring glad tidings to Zacharias (Luke 1:17). And then Gabriel came to Nazareth in Galilee where he appeared to Mary and told her that she had been favored and highly blessed of God. He told her that she would conceive a child and that His name would be Jesus (Luke 1:26–38).

> And behold, you will conceive in your womb and bring
> forth a Son, and shall call His name Jesus. He will be

great, and will be called the Son of the Highest; and
the Lord God will give Him the throne of His father
David. And He will reign over the house of Jacob forever, and of His kingdom there will be no end.
                                                —LUKE 1:31–33

Angels will be instrumental in the final judgment, and
they play important roles in fulfilling prophecy (Gen. 19; 2
Sam. 24:16; 2 Kings 19:35; Dan. 4:13, 17; Matt. 13:41–42,
47–50; Acts 12:23; Rev. 7:1–3; 8:2, 10–12; 10:1; 16:3–4).
They have great power (2 Pet. 2:11). Once, it took only one
angel to slay the entire Assyrian army of one hundred
eighty-five thousand men (2 Kings 19:35). We cannot
know the number of angels. We only get a hint of a perspective from the Bible: "More than twelve legions of
angels [this is somewhere between seventy-two thousand
and one hundred forty-four thousand]..." (Matt. 26:53).
"And I beheld an innumerable company of angels" (Heb.
12:22). "And I beheld and I heard the voice of many
angels...and the number of them was ten thousand times
ten thousand, and thousands and thousands" (Rev. 5:11).
    While Jesus walked and ministered on earth, angels
often attended Him (Matt. 2:19–20; 4:11; 25:31; 28:2–4;
Luke 22:43; 24:1–6; John 20:11–12; Acts 1:9–11). They
also sent forth to minister to God's servants, including us (1
Kings 19:5–8; Dan. 6:22; 10:10; Matt. 24:31; Luke 1:11, 26;
12:8; Acts 8:26; 10:3–6; 12:5–11; Heb.1:14; Rev. 21:9).
Angels marvel at sinners when they are saved (Luke 15:10).
They can never experience this redemption. They wonder
at us, since we were created a bit lower than the angels, but
raised in Christ Jesus to be higher (1 Cor. 4:9; Eph. 3:10; 1
Pet. 1:12). It was within the hierarchy of God's angels that
all terror and confusion began. There was an angel that was
very beautiful and intelligent; he was even called select.
This angel was named Lucifer (Ezek. 28:14). His job was to

61

guard the holiness of God. But Lucifer wanted to be God, and thus was cast from heaven. Since that time, he has reigned as the master of terror and confusion on earth.

Revelation 20:3 tells us that this angel deceives entire nations. He tries to hinder, snatch, distort and confuse the Word of God (Luke 8:12; 1 Thess. 2:18). He sows tares in and among the good wheat (Matt. 13:38–39). He incites persecution (Rev. 2:10).

One of Islam's major doctrinal themes embraces the belief in angels. They are said to abide in a supernatural realm. Legions of these angels are ministering types that do specific duties. There are also four archangels in Islam: Gabriel (messenger), Izrail (death angel), Israfil (angel of doom) and Michael (angel of providence). Islam also believes in the ousted angels of which Satan (Shatyan) is chief. *Jinn* are unusual and exotic spirits that live somewhere between the angels and mankind. They are mysterious and can be both evil and good.

Satan's angelic authority is extended and carried out by his many demons, also fallen angels. These demons are comprised of the other angels that followed his course of rebellion. The Bible tells us that Satan uses fallen angels as well as people to thwart the work of Jesus.

Satan and his angels dwell among us. They use and possess others to do evil work (Rev. 2:13). Satan possessed Judas to betray Jesus (John 13:27). And Muhammad was not influenced by Gabriel, but by the fallen angel. It is Satan that began the murderous work, and he is responsible for the shadowy scourge of Islam.

7

Women of Islam

But from the beginning of the creation, God "made them male and female. For this reason a man shall leave his father and mother and be joined to his wife, and the two shall become one flesh"; so then they are no longer two but one flesh. Therefore what God has joined together, let not man separate.

—MARK 10:6–9

This chapter is not intended to offend anyone. We must find truth. First and foremost, not all Muslim women are mistreated. Many are loved and cherished as mothers, wives, sisters, professionals, coworkers and friends. Many Muslims share the disgust with modern secular humanism, permissive, amoral and godless behavior, and they share a sense of moral repugnance at what our societies generally permit and sanction. We must reject media stereotypes and listen to the voice of the Holy Spirit.

We have a chance to help Muslims overcome their spiritual bondage. Satan dominates them through lies and intimidation. He bullies with rigid dictates. Nowhere is this more evident than in the pathetic condition of Muslim women in fundamentalist Islamic countries. In the Qur'anic sense an Islamic woman lives under the combination of excessive outward piety and under cruel bondage as a piece of property.

Under the strict authority of the Qur'an and Islamic law, men have authority over all women because Allah has made the one superior to the other and because they spend their wealth to maintain them. According to Sürah 4:34, good women are obedient. Women are dominated in Islam, as Muslim men feel powerful as duty compels the men to subdue and conquer the women. The humiliation of women under the extreme terrorists in Afghanistan is beyond appalling.

Women in fundamental Islamic enclaves are treated like subhuman slaves with astonishing cruelty and suppression, especially in places like Afghanistan, where they live in abject fear. Disobedience brings brutal punishment and often death. Women can have fingers or toes cut off if they wear nail polish, or they are publicly flogged. If they sin and have sex outside of marriage, they are simply murdered, often by a ruthless and heartless mob.

It is illegal for women to pluck their eyebrows or cut their hair short. They cannot wear makeup, stylish or colorful cloths, sheer stockings, white socks or high-heel shoes. They are forbidden from watching television, sports, talking loudly or laughing in the presence of men. Islamic men in Afghanistan carry broken car antennas and electric cables to whip women in the street should they catch them breaking any rule. The women must be covered from head to toe with the baglike garb called the *burqas*. One woman was beaten to death by an angry mob for accidentally exposing her arm. Often the windows of their home are painted from the outside so they can't be seen by the outside world. In countries like Afghanistan, controlled by Osama bin Laden and the Taliban, women who at one time made up 70 percent of the teachers and 40 percent of the doctors can no longer hold jobs or attend universities. Even their pictures cannot be displayed on walls or in newspapers or books. If they are raped and brutalized, there are generally no repercussions.

As one Islamic official put it, having a woman is like having a rose. You water it and keep it at home to look at and smell. It is not supposed to be taken out of the house to be smelled. Another leader put it this way: There are two places for women, at home and in the graveyard. One woman was shot for trying to rush her sick infant to the hospital without being accompanied by her husband or a male relative. Women die because they are not allowed to visit a male doctor. One woman bled to death on the steps of a hospital after a minor car accident as the male doctors watched. The infant mortality rate is off the charts.

In Islam women are to be kept in complete submission and are only here for bearing children and for the pleasure of men. Even in Islamic heaven, men are to be eternally pleasured by women called *houris*, who are beautiful young woman with transparent bodies. The marrow of a *houri's* bones is visible like the interior lines of pearls and rubies. She looks like red wine in a white glass. She is of white color and free from the routine physical disabilities of an ordinary woman, disabilities such as menstruation, menopause, urinal and offal discharge, child bearing and the related pollution. A *houri* is a girl of tender age, having large breasts that are round and not inclined to dangle. *Houris* dwell in palaces of splendid surroundings. If a *houri* looks down from her abode in heaven onto the earth, the whole distance shall be filled with light and fragrance, her face more radiant than a mirror, and one can see one's image in her cheek. The marrow of her shins is visible to the eyes. Every man who enters Jannah (paradise) shall be given seventy-two *houris*. No matter at what age he had died, when he is admitted into paradise, he will become a thirty-year-old and shall not age any further. Of course, a man in Jannah shall be given virility equal to that of one hundred men.[1]

Such sexual temptation drives the suicide bomber as he proceeds on his unholy quest. However, how can only seventy-two *houris* satisfy a warrior with a hundred men's virility? Once they tire of the *houris* in Jannah, they also find handsome young boys. There is no mention of married Muslim women in Jannah, even if they lived pious lives. Thus, wives, sisters and daughters of warriors cannot get inside Jannah. There is no mention made of where they will end up.

A Muslim man can have sexual pleasure with a child as young as a baby. However, he should not penetrate, although sodomizing the child is acceptable. If the man does penetrate and damage the child, he is then responsible for her subsistence all her life. This girl, however, does not count as one of his four permanent wives. The man will not be eligible to marry the girl's sister. It's better for a girl to marry in such a time when she would begin menstruation at her husband's house rather than her father's home. Any father marrying his daughter so young will have a permanent place in heaven.

A man can have sex with animals such as sheep, cows, camels and so on. However, he should kill the animal after he has his orgasm. He should not sell the meat to the people in his own village; however, selling the meat to the village next door should be fine.[2]

If a man commits sodomy with a cow, an ewe or a camel, their urine and their excrements become impure, and even their milk may no longer be consumed. The animal must then be killed and as quickly as possible and burned.[3]

Women of Afghanistan, under the strictest of Qur'anic dictates, are suffering under the most brutal antifeminine decrees and medieval punishments. Women are under virtual house arrest or set adrift in the streets like ghosts in a city of beggars to feed their children. The Taliban, meaning "students of Muslim religious studies," is mostly a gang of illiterate hooligans who have been brainwashed into such dictates by Mullah Mohammad Omar. Horrible stories continue to emerge following the World Trade Center bombings, where in Kabul alone there are thirty thousand homeless widows. Women and girls are dying of treatable inhumane conditions because they can't get medical care or can't afford a burqa.

Women who disobey behavioral codes are barbarically punished. Researchers have determined through hidden video cameras that the Taliban publicly punishes sinners in the Kabul sports stadium, requiring public attendance, with whippings, shootings, hangings, beheadings and the old stand-by, amputations.

Recently, the dilapidated stadium, which used to have soccer games, housed thirty thousand men and young boys for scheduled weekly entertainment. A young woman received one hundred lashes, and two thieves had their right hands cut off. The woman had been arrested for walking with a man not related to her, which was enough for her to be found guilty of adultery. Being single, her punishment was only flogging. Had she been married, she would have been stoned to death. Covered in the shroudlike burqa veil, she was forced to kneel. She was then whipped as the stadium rang with cheers. Physicians with surgical scalpels then carried out the amputations. Holding the severed hands by an index finger, a Taliban fighter warned the huge crowd of theft. To restore the party atmosphere, the thieves were driven around the stadium in a jeep, which precipitated a standing ovation. Again, the Qur'an was obeyed. The city's governor and a mullah said, "We have a lot of such unpunished cases, but the previous civil servants didn't have the courage to do what we are doing. These people have now been replaced, and these events will continue." Subsequently, the next scheduled program was announced, one stoning to death and three amputations.

Last March, the regime's only radio station permitted to operate broadcast that a young woman caught trying to flee Afghanistan with a man who was not her relative had been stoned to death. Two hundred twenty-five women had been rounded up and sentenced to a lashing for violating the dress code. The top of a woman's thumb was amputated for wearing nail polish. The regime claims they are restoring the purity of Islam.

The Qur'an teaches that a woman is to be covered in public with the traditional burqa. It is to cover the entire body save for the eyes, hands and feet. A heavy gauze patch across the eyes makes it hard to see and blocks peripheral vision. Vehicles have hit women because the burqa leaves them unable to walk fast or to see where they are going. The burqa now costs the equivalent of five months' salary; that is, if any women were still receiving one. Most cannot afford to buy the garment, and whole neighborhoods must share one. It can take several days for a woman's turn to come round; even if she has money to shop for food, she can't go out until then.

If a woman ventures out of her home, it must be for an Islamic-sanctioned purpose, and she must wear the burqa. A young mother was shot while taking her ill toddler to a doctor. Veiled, she was spotted by a Taliban guard, who tried to stop her. Afraid her child might die she kept going. The guard fired several rounds. She was hit, but she didn't die. Passersby watching the incident intervened, and she and her child received prompt medical attention. When her family complained, they were informed it was the injured woman's fault. She had no right being out in public in the first place.

The only public transport permitted women are special

buses, which are rarely available, that have all windows, except the driver's, covered with thick blankets. It is now illegal for women to talk to any men except close relatives, which precludes them from visiting male physicians, no matter how sick.

Women under the Taliban are severely depressed, and mental illness is growing at an alarming rate. Without the resources to leave the country, an increasing number are now choosing suicide, once rare, as a means of escape. Doctors are seeing a lot of esophageal burns. Women are swallowing battery acid or poisonous household cleansers because they are easy to find. It's a very painful way to die, but somehow preferred to life under the Taliban.

And why should women be so miserable?

The woman is considered low born and inferior. Islam categorizes her as having a very weak reasoning capacity, open to flattery and easily deceived. Women live under an extreme barrage of Qur'anic laws and regulations that include such matters as informing a mother not to have sex with her young son. A married woman can be stolen and made to remarry by a Muslim if she is a captive taken in *jihad*. Wives or concubines that disobey a man can be scourged and banished to beds apart from the man. They are to be most heavily admonished. Should a woman be caught in adultery, she can be confined to her house until she dies or she can be stoned to death.

> If any of your women commit fornication, call in four witnesses from among yourselves against them; if they testify to their guilt confine them to their houses till death overtakes them or till Allah finds another way for them.
>
> —SŪRAH 4:15

Men have authority over women because Allah has

made the one superior to the others, and because they
spend their wealth to maintain them. Good women
are obedient. They guard their unseen parts because
Allah has guarded them. Then if they obey you, take
no further action against them.

—SŪRAH 4:34

Marriage takes the form of a contract that effectuates its
validity merely in the essential presence of two free male
witnesses (Muslim, of course), or one man and another
man's equal, two women. A Muslim can marry a Jew or a
Christian (People of the Book). They may not marry a
polytheist or a Zoroastrian until they also become Muslims.
A non-Muslim's testimony is useless both in the propaga-
tion of a marriage or in its dissolution. A man can't marry
his wife's sister. He may not marry a slave after he is already
married to a free woman, but he can legally have four
wives. A male slave can marry only two women.
Muhammad, by special order from Allah, had fifteen. His
wives had a special status and are considered "the mothers
of all believers." Fundamentalists deem a woman unfit to
make any decisions or act as an agent for any contract. The
Qur'an teaches that a man must cohabit equally with his
wives if he has more than one. Should he be inclined to
favor one above the rest, he is subject to the judgment of
Allah. "The man who has two or more wives and who
inclines particularity to one of them shall on the day of
judgment be paralyzed on one side."[4]

A woman may not divorce a man for any reason, but the
man may divorce the woman merely on a whim. A man has
absolute power over a woman. The divorce can be consum-
mated when the woman is not menstruating and when it has
been determined that she is not with child. During this
period of waiting for the divorce to be finalized (*idda*), the
man is not to touch her. When he is ready to divorce, he

must simply state "I have divorced you" three times, and it is done. The man can reverse his decision if he so chooses.

Males are circumcised when they are very young, and in most fundamentalist schools, the women can be circumcised by clitoral excision. This is to keep them in bondage and to keep them from becoming too lusty. This can be done by the forceful command of the imam. A menstruating woman is prohibited from touching or reading the Qur'an, praying in the mosque, fasting, circumambulating holy places or sexual contact. A woman's only consolation is that she can't be divorced during this time. Besides four wives, a man may also have unlimited concubines as sexual cohorts. This domination carries over to heaven also.

> You are also forbidden to take in marriage women, except captives whom you own as slaves. Such is the decree of Allah. All women other than these are lawful to you, provided you seek them with your wealth in modest conduct, not in fornication. Give them their dowry for the enjoyment you have had of them as a duty; but it shall be no offense to you to make any agreement among yourselves after you have fulfilled your duty. Allah is wise and all-knowing.
>
> —SÜRAH 4:24

In public a woman is not to even look at a man. She is always to worship from the back of the mosque, or better yet, in a separate room. She can't drive a car or work in a government office. Until the mid-fifties women could not go to school, though that is changing in some countries. There are many women in Islamic countries that are kept hidden by wealthy men. They are taken when very young and are never seen by the outside world. They are kept in their quarters and never allowed out of them.

8

Basic Islam

> But there were also false prophets among the people, even as there will be false teachers among you, who will secretly bring in destructive heresies, even denying the Lord who brought them…and many will follow their destructive ways, because of whom the way of truth will be blasphemed.
>
> —2 PETER 2:1–2

Islam literally means submission or surrender. It is a monotheistic religion that stresses the brotherhood (*ummah*) of all men and nations ultimately yoked together under Qur'anic law. This community's sole purpose is to fulfill the human obligation and say yes to the Qur'an. The emphasis is on belief in Allah and his dictates as dispensed by Muhammad. The only acceptable counterbalance is heresy or unbelief, which carries with it the sentence of death.

The Muslim states, "Allah Akbar," which means, "Allah alone is great." To become a Muslim one need only repeat, "La ilaha, il'Allah, Muhammadan and Raoula Allah." This confession of faith affirms that Allah is the only God and that Muhammad is his messenger.

Islam is the world's fastest-growing religion. Proliferation is encouraged, and the average birth rate is six children per woman.[1] Born in the Arabian interior early in the seventh century, it has become a major religion with over one hundred fifty sects. Most estimates maintain the population to be near one billion, or approaching one-fourth of the earth's inhabitants.

There are over eighty countries in which Islam makes up at least 2 percent of the population, and thirty-nine where it makes up more than half. Over one hundred languages are spoken throughout these countries. Persian, Turkish, Arabic, Indian and Indonesian are the major dialects.

Muslims are found in a variety of lands. But much of this land is desolate desert waste that silently surrounds barren volcanic steppes. These sand seas hold hardly any surface water. The Muslim population lives in these lands that stretch along both sides of the equator from Morocco to the Philippines. The greatest concentration is in the Indian subcontinent, primarily Pakistan, Bangladesh and Indonesia.

The Muslims live in great contrasts. Semi-primitive Bedouin nomads herd sheep next to state-of-the-art oil refineries. A Rolls-Royce may be found parked next to a remote goatskin tent. Some search endlessly for life-giving water in the barren forbidding lands, while still others live in overpopulated urban trading centers. Life varies from abject poverty of the sparse farming clans to the mega-rich royalty, who enjoy billions from the underground reservoirs of oil.

Islam resurfaced with a purposeful vengeance in the twentieth century. Fueled by the petro dollars of black gold and a growing sense of unity, it sluggishly and grudgingly caught up to the twentieth century from a medieval existence. Allah condones and encourages economic success. It is the opinion in the Mideast that they were given the vast reservoirs of oil so that they could eventually achieve world superiority and destroy the unbelieving infidels.

Unlike the idolaters before him, Muhammad preached one God. He did well, for this conviction is the cornerstone of the Old Testament. "Hear, O Israel: The LORD our God, the LORD is one!" (Deut. 6:4). This is not remarkable, for Satan himself believes in one God: "You believe that there is one God. You do well. Even the demons believe—and tremble!" (James 2:19).

Fundamentalist Islam, as found in the Qur'an, is not tolerant of other religions. The Qur'an actually forbids equitable coexistence. People of different faiths have no rights in predominant Islamic countries and live at great risk. There are few Christian churches allowed—and none in Afghanistan. Its sole purpose is to deny the deity of Jesus. The Qur'an ordains, "Give the warning to those in whose (hearts) is the fear that they will be brought (to Judgment) before their Lord: except for Him they will have no protector nor intercessor" (Sürah 6:51).

> They say: "(Allah) Most Gracious has begotten a son!" Indeed ye have put forth a thing most monstrous! As if the skies are ready to burst, the earth to split asunder, and the mountains to fall down in utter ruin, that they should invoke a son for (Allah) Most Gracious.
>
> —SÜRAH 19:88–91

The Qur'an says that no one can intercede for a person. Everyone is on their own. The deity of Jesus, or "Isa" as the Qur'an calls Him, is considered blasphemy.

> Then Allah will say: Jesus, Son of Mary, did you ever say to mankind: Worship Me and My mother as gods

beside Allah? Glory to you He will answer, how could I say that to which I have no right? You know what is in My mind, but I cannot tell you what is in yours. You alone know what is hidden. I spoke to them nothing except what you bade Me. I said: Serve Allah, My Lord and your Lord.

—Sūrah 5:116–117

Muhammad stressed that neither he nor any angel from heaven was in possession of the secrets of Allah. "I tell you not that with me are the treasures of Allah, nor do I know what is hidden" (Sūrah 6:50).

The point of no available savior is most heavily stressed in the Qur'an. The intention is to remove the salvation of Jesus from humanity. But all biblical prophecy leads to the fulfillment of Jesus as our Savior. Scripture says we are complete in Him and that Jesus did possess the attributes of God: "In whom are hidden all the treasures of wisdom and knowledge. Now this I say lest anyone should deceive you with persuasive words" (Col. 2:3–4).

Jesus told the unbelievers, "You know neither Me nor My Father. If you had known Me, you would have known My Father... You are from beneath; I am from above. You are of this world; I am not of this world" (John 8:19, 23).

Without Jesus souls are easy prey for the wiles of Satan. The Bible tells us that no one can attain salvation without Jesus. No principles or determinations, no matter how sublime, can replace God's scriptural plan for salvation. It is written in the Bible, "Nor is there salvation in any other, for there is no other name given among men by which we must be saved" (Acts 4:12).

The Qur'an commands its followers to work for their salvation. This is the same doctrine of karma yoga (working for salvation) that originated in the Far Eastern scriptures of the idol worshipers. Only by following the prescribed duties as outlined by Muhammad can a Muslim be saved. But the Bible teaches us that no man has the power over life and death; neither can anyone overcome the world by himself or herself. We have access to this salvation because God loved us (John 3:16). The apostle Paul wrote, "For by grace you have been saved through faith, and that not of yourselves; it is the gift of God, not of works, lest anyone should boast" (Eph. 2:8–9).

Islam not only tries to snatch our salvation, but it also reduces Jesus, who is God Himself, to the status of just another prophet. Muslims are deceived. Jesus is the Allah Muslims seek. Islam claims that Muhammad was greater than Jesus. It teaches that Muhammad came with a superior revelation and the final word of all prophets. It calls Muhammad the seal of the prophets. For this reason Islam also goes to great lengths to portray Muhammad as a mere man. It categorizes Jesus as inferior to him, but inexplicably hints at the contradictory notion that intercession is one of the privileges of the Messiah (Sürah 3:45).

There are many accounts of Jesus, His messiahship, His miracles and even His virgin birth in the Qur'an. It says that Jesus had the ability to heal and raise people from the dead; it also claims He created a bird from the dust (Sürah 3:49; 5:110). Of course, it stresses that this was done only through Allah's permission and that Jesus is not God. There are many such accounts, many of which are not even in the Bible. Some can be traced to pseudo gospels.

The Qur'an says that Jesus was born with John among the children of Israel into the house of Imran. Curiously, Jesus is mentioned ninety-seven times in the Qur'an, Muhammad but twenty-five. To associate Jesus with Allah (God) is blasphemy and the most grievous sin in Islam.

Jesus is compared to Adam in the Qur'an:

Lo! The likeness of Jesus with Allah is as the likeness of

Adam, O Muhammad! They have blasphemed who have said that Allah is Christ the Son of Mary. Then Muhammad replied, O Gabriel! They ask me to tell them to whom Isa [Jesus] is similar, and Gabriel said, Isa is just as Adam in the sight of Allah. He created Him of dust and then said to Him be and He was. This is the truth from your lord: therefore do not doubt it. To those that dispute with you concerning Jesus after the knowledge you have received, say: Come; let us gather our sons and your sons, our wives and your wives, our people and your people. We will pray together and call down the curse of Allah on every liar. This is the whole truth. There is no God but Allah.

—SÜRAH 3:59–62

A key verse in the Qur'an is:

People of the Book [Bible] do not go too far in your religion, and say nothing about Allah but the truth. The Messiah, Jesus Son of Mary, was only a messenger of Allah, and His word He committed to Mary and a Spirit from Him. So believe in Allah and his messengers and say not: There! Refrain! Better is it for you. They worship their rabbis and their monks, and the Messiah, the Son of Mary, as gods besides Allah; though they were ordered to serve only One God only. There is no God but Allah.

—SÜRAH 9:31; 4:154–159

Islam holds that Mary conceived Jesus without any human relationship and that she was faultless. She was to have borne Him near a tree and then taken Him to her family. They looked upon her with the disdain of a prostitute. The Qur'an says Jesus was infallible, full of wisdom and with supernatural knowledge. As an infant, Jesus

77

explained to them that He is Allah's servant: "Lo! I am a slave of Allah. He hath given Me scripture and hath appointed Me a prophet" (Sürah 19:22–36).

We find in the Bible quite a different story: "For unto us a Child is born, unto us a Son is given; and the government will be upon His shoulder. And His name will be called Wonderful, Counselor, Mighty God, Everlasting Father, Prince of Peace. Of the increase of His government and peace, there will be no end" (Isa. 9:6–7).

The Bible tells us that God came to us in the flesh. "In the beginning was the Word, and the Word was with God, and the Word was God…And the Word was made flesh and dwelt among us" (John 1:1, 14).

Islam conceals, distorts and disavows the victory of Jesus by denying His death and His resurrection. His crucifixion is denied because Islam teaches that there was no collective guilt to atone for. They teach that the cross holds no significance because man is born sinless. They say that Jesus was rejected, but that Allah simply took Him to Himself.

To support the contention that men were born sinless and that there is no need for a Savior, Islam does away with original sin. Because mankind has not incurred this sin, they say they can make salvation on their own. Adam's fall is not seen as sin, but it is simply dismissed as an error in human judgment. But it is written: "All we like sheep have gone astray; we have turned, every one, to his own way; and the LORD has laid on Him the iniquity of us all" (Isa. 53:6).

Scripture tells us that all the great prophets sinned. The apostles sinned. The Qur'an tells us that Muhammad sinned (Sürah 33:36–38; 47:19). Jesus Christ was sinless, a lamb without blemish, the perfect sacrifice. It is written:

> If we say that we have no sin, we deceive ourselves, and the truth is not in us. If we confess our sins, He is faithful and just to forgive us our sins and to cleanse

us from all unrighteousness. If we say that we have not
sinned, we make Him a liar, and His word is not in us.
—1 JOHN 1:8–9

Satan wants to muddle and steal away that which was
wrought on Calvary. He has determined that someone else
died in Jesus' place, or other Islamic fables have it that Jesus
had the ability to cast His likeness on another. "When
Allah said: O Jesus! Lo! I am fathering you and causing you
to ascend to me, and am cleansing you of those who believe
and am setting those who follow thee above those who dis-
believe until the day of Resurrection. Then unto me you
will return and I shall judge between you as to that wherein
you used to differ" (Sürah 3:55).

The Qur'an also states, "That they said (in boast), 'We
killed Christ Jesus the son of Mary, the Apostle of God';
but they killed him not, nor crucified him, but so it was
made to appear to them, and those who differ therein are
full of doubts, with no certain knowledge, but only conjec-
ture to follow, for of a surety they killed him not—nay,
Allah raised him up unto Himself; and Allah is Exalted in
Power, Wise" (Sürah 4:157–158).

But, again, we find that the Bible has an altogether different rendition of truth. Mary, His mother, Mary
Magdalene and His beloved disciple John all stood at the
foot of the cross on that fateful day. The sky was darkened,
the earth shook and the veil in the holy of holies was rent
in two. Surely His most intimate followers recognized their
beloved Master. Surely His own mother knew her Son.

Paul wrote:

> For I delivered to you first of all that which I also
> received: that Christ died for our sins according to the
> Scriptures, and that He was buried, and that He rose
> again the third day according to the Scriptures, and

that He was seen by Cephas and then by the twelve. After that He was seen by over five hundred brethren at once.

—1 CORINTHIANS 15:3–6

Jesus Himself affirmed His messiahship and the fact that He would die and rise again. All the prophecies and Gospel writers embrace and agree with prophecy and Jesus' predictions (Gen. 3:15; Ps. 22; Isa. 53:5, 7, 9; Zech. 12:10; Matt. 17:22–23; 26:14–15; 27:3–8, 34, 42; Mark 8:31; 15:1–42; John 3:14–16; 19:30–42; Rev.1:17–18). Matthew wrote, "From that time Jesus began to show His disciples that He must go to Jerusalem, and suffer many things from the elders and chief priests and scribes, and be killed, and be raised again the third day" (Matt. 16:21). And it happened!

Who, when He was reviled, did not revile in return; when He suffered, He did not threaten, but committed Himself to Him who judges righteously; who Himself bore our sins in His own body on the tree, that we, having died to sins, might live for righteousness—by whose stripes you were healed.

—1 PETER 2:23–24

Over and over again the Qur'an insists Jesus was but a prophet: "And (Jesus) shall be a Sign (for the coming of) the Hour (of Judgment): therefore have no doubt about the (Hour), but follow ye Me: this is a Straight Way" (Sürah 43:61).

According to Islamic tradition, Jesus is called the Herald of the Last Judgment. He is to come back, but only to destroy Christianity and what Islam calls its idolatrous church. Again, the Bible tells an altogether different story. It calls the church Jesus' bride and says He is coming back for it. This church is born of His Spirit. A Christian is born into and lives within this body. This church is one with Jesus as a bride is one with her husband. The real Christian church beckons all souls to safety. It is written:

> "I, Jesus, have sent My angel to testify to you these things in the churches. I am the Root and the Offspring of David, the Bright and Morning Star." And the Spirit and the bride say, "Come!" And let him who hears say, "Come." And let him who thirsts come. Whoever desires, let him take the water of life freely.
>
> —REVELATION 22:16–17

9

A War Called Jihad

For we do not wrestle against flesh and blood, but
against principalities, against powers, against the
rulers of the darkness of this age, against spiritual
hosts of wickedness in the heavenly places.

—Ephesians 6:10

As the world gears up for the first war of the twenty-
first century, terrorism will force America and her
alliance into uncharted waters against an amor-
phous enemy. The war is against terror, which is defined as
the unlawful use or threatened use of force or violence by a
person or organized group against people or property with
the intention of intimidating or coercing societies, religions
or governments, often for ideological or political reasons.

Terrorism comes in many guises, from deadly poisons
to propaganda to bombs. Jets filled with highly flammable
aviation fuel were hijacked and flown into the Pentagon
and the Twin Towers of the World Trade Center.
Powerful car bombs explode in crowded market places.
Terrorists with bombs strapped to their persons walk into

gatherings and detonate. School buses have been shot at and bombed. Broken glass and jagged metal whiz mercilessly through thick hot smoke. People panic and scream. Blood splatters everywhere, the crimson liquid spreading across walls and oozing along concrete. For the moment, death and terror reign.

In another part of the world, an altogether different cry is heard. The radical fundamentalist Muslim gives praise to Allah, the god he serves. He sincerely thanks him for the successful carnage. As the terrorist confers praises on the god of his fathers, he is respected and honored for his decisive work. He has been obedient. He has killed infidels (unbelievers). He has applied *jihad*. The Qur'an's injunctions have again rocketed across the globe. Its ferocious position and reputation have expanded. Satan is pleased. The fundamentalist Muslim has been faithful to the Qur'an. He has done the will of the false god it conceals and thereby insured himself a place with him.

These have become all-too-typical scenarios in today's world. Back during the Christmas season of 1988, Pan Am flight 103 was blown out of the sky over Scotland as it made its way from Heathrow Airport. A well-known terrorist organization proudly took the credit as families mourned the loss of loved ones and helplessly asked why. But the terrorist threat was still not taken that seriously. And now, a great tragedy on American shores has given the world a true vision of *jihad* and its steadfast campaign of terror. Serve me or die! Reject the deity of Jesus or die! Become a Muslim or die! Leave our land or die!

The terrorist organizations have many independent cells around the world preparing to sustain this *jihad*. They chasten mankind to submit to Islam or expect more of the same. The sentiment runs deep as many Islamic elite secretly support terrorism through clandestine banking systems, while they conveniently ply the Qur'anic injunction of pretending to be friends with the enemy until they are strong enough to kill him.

Some scholars teach that *jihad* is purely a spiritual struggle, a wrestling match against the evil tendencies of one's own human soul. But Muhammad Saleh explained, "*Jihad* is a code term. Killing your enemy is positive." He, like the majority of Muslim scholars, consider *jihad* to be a compulsory obligation in the Qur'an: "Fighting is prescribed for you, and ye dislike it" (Sürah 2:216).

The concept of *jihad* developed gradually. At first, Muhammad did not have the army to dominate and coerce people into Islam. But eventually, good fortune fell into his lap, and just as in Adolph Hitler's case, his persistence paid off. For political reasons, a group of feuding Arabs in Medina accepted him as their prophet. They hoped he could help them maintain peace. They eventually made a pledge to support Muhammad in war against the Quraysh.[1]

It was only when Muhammad had a strong enough following that could defend themselves, when his people were migrating north to Medina and when he knew he was going to leave town, that suddenly Allah gave Muhammad his revelation to fight. As circumstances changed, Muhammad's Allah changed with them. Muhammad methodically went from only warning the nonbelievers to being an aggressor. Muhammad's trusted follower Zeyd was assailed while evangelizing. He struck a person with a camel goad and drew blood. Shortly thereafter Muhammad addressed many verses to the faithful in support of bloodshed. When Muhammad and his followers had attacked a caravan and killed its leader Abu Jahl, he proclaimed that he was more pleased with the head that was cast at his feet than if someone had given him a select camel.

As a result, Muhammad fashioned such a verse: "The punishment of those who wage war against Allah and His Apostle, and strive with might and main for mischief through the land is: execution, or crucifixion, or the cutting off of hands and feet from opposite sides, or exile from the land" (Sürah 5:33).

Killing nonbelievers is not at all a new phenomenon in Islam. At Medina the first person to be killed was a woman. She had composed poetic verses that ridiculed Muhammad and his followers. She said Muhammad was a debaucher and a murderer. A blind man named 'Umair swore that he would kill her. While she slept, he put a sword through her chest. When 'Umair told Muhammad of what he had done, Muhammad replied, "Behold a man that hath assisted the Lord and his prophet. Call him not blind, call him rather 'Umair, the seeing."[2]

In Medina, Muhammad had conflicts with the Jews and pagans. The first murder recorded involves Muhammad's command to his followers to kill Jews.[3] Muhammad said, "Kill any Jew that falls into your power." Upon this command Muhayyisa Masud leapt upon Ibn Sunayna, a Jewish merchant with whom he had social and business relations, and killed him. When Muhayyisa killed him, his elder brother Huwayyisa began to beat him, saying, "You enemy of God, why did you kill him when much of the fat on your belly comes from his wealth?" Muhayyisa answered, "Had the one who ordered me to kill him ordered me to kill you I would have cut your head off."[4] Note that this Muslim murderer would have killed a family member at the drop of a hat.

> It's remarkable that Islamic tradition attribute Muhammad's most cruel acts to divine order, namely the siege of Qaynuqa, the murder of Kab, and his attack upon Qurayzah. Allah's conscience seems to be more elastic than that of his creatures.[5]

The second murder victim was Abu Afak, who had urged his fellow Medinans to question Muhammad.[6] Muhammad said, "Who will deal with this rascal for me?" Abu Afak, a Jewish man of great age (reputedly one hundred twenty years), was killed because he had lampooned Muhammad. Salem Omayr did the deed at the behest of the Prophet. The killing of such an old man moved a poetess, Asma Marwan, to compose disrespectful verses about the Prophet. She too was assassinated. Thus Muhammad gradually transformed Islam from a purely spiritual mission into a militant and punitive organization whose progress depended on booty from raids and revenue from the *zakat* (tax).

Islam can be a very militant faith and will resort to violent *jihad* to defend itself or promote its objectives. These murders represent what Muhammad was all about. The methodology is to kill and terrorize those who are a threat to your credibility and the spread of Islam. "I will instill terror into the hearts of the Unbelievers: Smite ye above their necks and smite all their finger-tips off them" (Sürah 8:12).

The vast majority of Arabs worldwide instinctively know that militancy and killing are wrong. Not even the ayatollahs and mullahs of Iran were able to inspire the Iranian people with the spirit of *jihad* to the extent they wanted. Although the population of Iran is three times that of Iraq, Saddam Hussein was still able to put more men into battle than Khomeini. But Islam preaches *jihad*, and a good Muslim is expected to participate.

Only the dictates of the Qur'an are tolerated. A Muslim man named Foda asked a question about a Muslim dispute whether men in paradise would have erections, but merely protracted, not perpetual. "Is this what concerns Muslims at the end of the twentieth century?" he asked in a magazine column. "The world around us is busy with the conquest of space, genetic engineering and the wonders of the computer, while Muslim scholars," he wrote in sadness and pain, "were worried about sex in paradise." He was killed.

Let us plunge into the deeper reality of *jihad* beyond the

surface struggles for a Palestinian homeland and humanistic causes given as justification. The greater battle is for the souls of mankind. *Jihad* is far more than the indiscriminate violence we witness. It's the required mentality for all Muslims, and Satan patrols the Islamic corridors to insure continued compliance. To understand events in the Middle East one must understand the spiritual underpinnings of *jihad*. *Jihad* is to Islam as love is to Christianity. It is the standard above all else. Everything a Muslim is required to do is *jihad*. *Jihad* is designed to encourage complete submission to the Qur'an and Muhammad, the prophet of Allah.

Whether a person is removed from Jesus by the point of a sword or enticed by jingling heavenly prose, it is called *jihad*. Those that try to humanize Islam refer to the nonviolent aspects. They call *jihad* comprehensive, a term difficult to define. As we focus on the Qur'an, the true meaning will become quite clear. *Jihad* is to further the aim of Muhammad and remove Jesus as Savior. *Jihad* is worse than death of the body for it fosters eternal damnation. If one is a sincere follower of the fundamental Qur'anic verses, one practices *jihad*. It is the unbending credo of a god brought to bear by the angel of light (Satan) and his mad prophet (Muhammad).

There is no freedom of speech in Islam. Islamic adherents have called Salman Rushdie, born a Muslim in Bombay, a renegade apostate and a heretic. In his fictional book *The Satanic Verses*, Mr. Rushdie expresses skepticism about the authenticity of the so-called revealed word in the Qur'an. For this he is condemned to death. Also, anyone in any way associated with the book's publication is sentenced to death. Understandably, Rushdie, with the cooperation of Scotland Yard, went into hiding.

Mr. Rushdie's offense was to point out Muhammad's obvious contradictory and self-serving instructions, and thereby suggest that Muhammad could be capable of human error. Through a series of dream sequences,

Rushdie challenges Islam in a flighty, irreverent, whimsical and sometimes outrageous way. His playful and sometimes inadvertent parody makes many crafty suggestions concerning Muhammad (Mahound, as the book calls him). He questions the status of the angel that supposedly delivered the message of Islam to him.

Rushdie's novel was met with book burnings, bookstore bombings, killing, riots and a six-million-dollar contract on his life issued by the extreme fundamentalist the Ayatollah Khomeini. Nations broke diplomatic relations with Iran as a consequence of this barbaric edict. The Ayatollah Khomeini, Iran's late spiritual leader, said of Mr. Rushdie: "This man has no choice but to die because he has confronted a billion Muslims and the Imam."[7]

According to Islam, Mr. Rushdie sinned against *hodud* (the limits of Islamic propriety). Consequently, he is sentenced to death by full command of the imam. Whoever kills him is guaranteed the status of martyrdom and promised to go directly to heaven.[8]

The terrorist activity and the death threats are not just the dictates of some off-the-wall crazed madman, nor do they stem from one country. They spread from universal Islamic religious doctrine and directly from the pages of the Qur'an. *Jihad* involves fundamental Islamic law. It is as fundamental as the commandment to "love your neighbor" in the Bible. The Ayatollah who directed the death threats is simply a devout fundamentalist and uncompromising follower of the Qur'an. As long as such men worship and obey the dictates of the god that brought the Qur'an to bear, they must terrorize and kill infidels with *jihad*.

Recently I visited briefly with a missionary assigned to a particular Muslim country. He was burdened to bring the gospel to the Muslim people. He had already been instrumental in converting eighteen thousand to the love of Jesus Christ. He related the story of a dear friend of his who had been a doctor. This man initially met with the missionary only because he wanted help in getting a visa to Canada. He wished to find a greater opportunity and escape the harsh conditions in his country. But after he met the missionary and learned about the gospel of Jesus Christ, he accepted Jesus as his Savior. Shortly thereafter, while peacefully sleeping, he was stabbed to death.

This is not an uncommon or isolated incident in such countries. The new convert was killed because of a specific tenet of *jihad.* Strict Islamic law teaches that anyone who leaves or denounces Islam is to be immediately killed. Muslims believe that they have been given the final revelation and are called upon to enforce Allah's will in the final days. As the fundamentalist furor grows, many more such deaths will occur. On the other hand, if one converts to Islam, he is given immediate status of brotherhood.

Most Muslim countries still refuse to sign the charter for human rights because it grants people the right to change religions. Christian endeavors are strictly forbidden. Another missionary, this one from Great Britain, told me that many churches in Europe are now being turned into mosques. The spreading darkness is designed to destroy the deity of Jesus and remove any hope of mankind.

Today we find many ruthless state-sponsored terrorist organizations backed by many countries. Within the El-Fatah is Yasir Arafat's group. Abu Nidal, who surfaced within El-Fatah, was considered by most intelligence agencies to be one of the most dangerous, brazen and successful terrorists alive. In the West German weekly *Der Spiegel,* Abu Nidal stated, "I am the evil spirit of the secret services. I am the evil spirit which moves around only at night causing them nightmares."

The charter of the Palestine Armed Resistance describes their national duty as an irreversible firm *jihad* as the only way to free their homeland. The struggle is *jihad,* and as the

Qur'an instructs, it is to go on at any price and under any circumstance. The Palestinians assume the Qur'anic posture that they own Israel and are the rightful heirs to it. Covert commando tactics and bombings are the norm for these groups, and all other solutions or substitutes are to be rejected.[9]

Yasir Arafat was quoted as saying, "Palestine fell in a storm of fire and lead, and as is known, lead has no ideology. Our principles are guns pointed at the enemy's chests. We derive our ideas from mines."[10]

Unfortunately, most governments until now did not recognize the tangible depth and actual spiritual nature of these hostile organizations. They were only viewed and described as having distinctive political ideologies. But these groups carry the fundamental torch of Islam. They are the inner core, the heartbeat and the very essence of Islam.

The social order, the law, the religious structure and the army of *jihad* are identical. The Arab Muslim is on top of this social order, followed by slaves (*dhimnis*) and then prisoners. Any infidel or Christian whose life is spared is given status below that of a slave. In the business world or political arena all but Muslims are viewed as infidels to be dealt with as dogs and slaves. Slaves are considered a gift from Allah.

Muhammad himself participated in this militaristic quest of *jihad*. Clad in armor, he fought in at least nine battles and ordered many more. He was directly or indirectly involved in over sixty-five battles. During his lifetime Muhammad set the stage for *jihad's* continuance by transforming the vagrant superstitious tribesmen into superb desert warriors. Being greatly influenced by Alexander the Great, the ambitious Muhammad left these words: "One prophet, one faith for all the world."

Muhammad generated this verse that ordered him to fight: "So fight, Muhammad, for the cause of Allah. You are accountable for no one but yourself. Rouse the faithful: perchance Allah will defeat the unbelievers. He is mightier and more truculent than they" (Sürah 4:84).

The major principle of *jihad* is that a Muslim is either to convert an infidel to Islam or he must kill him. There is no other option. With Muhammad's growing prominence, beheading, butchery, torture and death became common-place. "It is not for any prophet to have prisoners until he has made wide slaughter in the land" (Sürah 8:68). "Prophet, make war on the unbelievers and the hypocrites and deal sternly with them. Hell shall be their home, evil their fate" (Sürah 66:9).

All prophets and martyrs are considered exempt of final judgment according to the Qur'an. Should warriors die during the exercise of *jihad*, they are told they will go directly to heaven. In light of this absolution, it clearly behooves a Muslim to go to war or to pursue a suicidal course of action. Fundamentalist Islam uses this lie to fill its ranks with impassioned extremists, many under the age of twelve. The Qur'an says, "All who die fighting in the ways of Allah are richly rewarded, while those who draw back will be punished" (Sürah 48:16–17).

There are only two houses in Islam: *Dar al-Islam*, the house of believers, and *Dar al-Harb*, the house of war. All nonbelievers are to be kept in the house of war. Terrorism will exist as long as there is one person who faithfully prac-tices the religion of fundamental Islam and one person who does not submit to it.

The Qur'an says, "The believers who stay home apart from those who suffer from a great impediment are not equal to those who fight for the cause of Allah with their goods and their persons. Allah has given those that fight with their goods and persons higher rank that those that stay home. He has promised all a reward; but far wider is the recompense of those who fight for him. Let those who would exchange the life of this world for the hereafter, fight for the cause of Allah; whether they die or conquer, he shall richly reward them" (Sürah 4:95).

Muhammad said, "Shall I not tell you of the peak of the matter, its pillar, and the topmost part? The peak is Islam, the pillar is prayer and its topmost part is *jihad*."

Jihad is an ongoing effort. The war effort is to cease only long enough to garner supplies or to fill ranks. Peace is considered but a time for preparation. One warrior simply hits the hammer softly while another swings it wildly.

According to the Qur'an, war can be the only relationship between a Muslim and his neighbor. A Muslim is to do business with infidels only until enough money or momentum is generated for an all-out attack against him. The provision that allows a Muslim to even do business with an infidel is that it must be done with the ulterior motive of eventually killing him. Should any Muslim disagree or fall in with an infidel, a similar fate of death awaits him.

Such provisions of *jihad* may remind us of Anwar Sadat, who had gotten a bit too cozy with the ways of the West. In 1981 religious zealots viciously assassinated him. His dream of achieving a peaceful coexistence with Israel and the United States was shattered. The imam said that he died because he associated with Christian and Jewish dogs.

The Shah of Iran too had dreams. He wanted to make Iran the Japan of the Middle East and became an ally of the United States. What the fundamentalists viewed as careless puppet-like collaboration cost him his country. The Muslim brotherhood danced in the streets when he died and celebrated the fact that fundamentalist Islam was not broken down. In the fundamental sense, any Muslim that deals with the West for any reason except *jihad* is to be killed. A Muslim is to also accept death before a Christian or a Jew rules him.

As for the unbelievers, alike it is for them whether thou hast warned them, for they do not believe. Allah has set a seal upon their hearts and on their hearing; and on their eyes is a covering, and there awaits for them a mighty chastisement.

—Sūrah 2:6

In 1979, following the rule of the Shah of Iran, the Ayatollah Khomeini returned to Iran from exile in Paris. He was hailed as a savior of Islam. He declared that Islam is the religion of Allah's freedom fighters. All who did not comply were killed. Supporters of the Shah were tortured and exterminated by the thousands. The Ayatollah pronounced, "The purest joy in Islam is to kill or be killed for Allah."[1]

Iran accommodates various Al Jihad squads affectionately called Al Mujahedeen. They are brutal and relentless. The Qur'an declares that it is to be an Islamic world or it is death! Like an uncontrollable forest fire, the fundamentalist furor has grown since the Western ideals were overthrown in Iran and Egypt. The three great Muslim empires that fell due to the Renaissance, the New World and the Industrial Revolution are again on the rise. Islamic studies are now compulsory in many countries. Every child must learn Qur'an and begin *jihad*. Civil servants must wear Islamic dress, and women must be covered from head to foot with the traditional burqa. This too is *jihad*.

Between the last two world wars, pressure had already been building to free the Arab countries from foreign dominance. The present awakening originated from this movement. During this time Jama al-Din, sometimes called al-Afgani, traveled throughout the Islamic world urging revolution. He was a thorn in the side of British monarchy and fostered many assassinations. Today his call has matured to a worldwide effort. Return to foreign domination is no longer conceivable. I believe the Russians have found this determination and resolve to be correct in Afghanistan, as did the Americans in Iran and Egypt.

Muhammad had begun his conquests by persuasion, teaching and preaching. Curiously, he originally said he was only asked to call men to Allah, to bear insult and to forgive the ignorant. But he was ridiculed, ill treated and accused of being a liar and a lunatic. As his forces grew larger and more formidable, his tactics changed. He said Allah changed his mind. Soon he began to take the infidels by the sword. Islam spread quickly because the only initial resistance was from small and impoverished desert clans. Muhammad cited the rapid expansion of his army as proof of his divine authority.

> Remember how the Unbelievers plotted against thee, to keep thee in bonds, or slay thee, or get thee out (of thy home). They plot and plan, and Allah too plans, but the best of planners is Allah.
> —SÜRAH 8:30

During the course of *jihad*, Muhammad used economic incentives to spur on the faithful. In fact, the early success could be easily attributed to the newly kindled appetites of the destitute desert dwellers rather than religion. And as for Muhammad, he became merely a conquering madman spouting new verses when it struck his fancy.

Muhammad left behind these words: "Prophets, rouse the faithful to arms. If there are twenty steadfast men among you, you shall vanquish two hundred; and if there are one hundred, they shall route a thousand unbelievers, for they are devoid of understanding" (Sürah 8:65).

By developing *jihad*, Muhammad steered masses of humanity toward bondage to Islam or annihilation. He did whatever was necessary to make people accept the dictates of his spiritual experience. He methodically assembled an army for Allah militarily, by diplomacy, by banditry or by whatever means were at his disposal. Muhammad was the arm of chastisement in the religion of death. There are far too many examples of the subsequent slaughter and devastation to elucidate upon here.

Even the Qur'an admits, "Generations before you We destroyed when they did wrong: their Apostles came to them with Clear Signs, but they would not believe! Thus do We requite those who sin!" (Sürah 10:13).

Just a few decades ago, illiterate Islamic hordes, enticed by spoil, swept into what was India and now Pakistan. They looted, ravaged and demolished the mansions, pilfered the temples and converted them into mosques. Indian men were tortured to convert, and the women were raped. The young boys and girls were sold into slavery. Many Indian women were said to have committed suicide when they saw the ruthless Muslims approach.

When one reads the Islamic account, there is an altogether different story: It recalls the glorious centuries of *jihad* when Allah blessed them with idol-worshiping India for their own. The marauder was raised to sainthood who to the Indian was but a terrorist and a murderer.

All the non-Muslim Indians were looked upon as dogs and swine and considered but cannon fodder. The death toll rose so high that history only leaves estimates. All buildings were taken over and were communicated in writing to have Muslim origins. Any men that were spared had to pay a tax (*jizya*) and wear a patch so that no Muslim would ever pay them any respect.

Any Jews or Christian allowed to live in Islamic lands are considered slaves and must also pay this tax. It is paid in exchange for protection and as sort of a tribute. In this way Christian and Jewish slaves are made to help finance *jihad*. This heavy tribute is expected in lieu of military service.

Thanks are in order for Jesus who took *jihad* to the cross.

As the sea of darkness spreads, a true Lighthouse is needed. All who take refuge in the mighty name of Jesus will find refuge from this scourge. Christianity does not condone the idolatry of India, but Jesus has an entirely different approach.

> You have heard it said, "You shall love your neighbor and hate your enemy." But I say to you, love your enemies, bless those who curse you, do good to those who hate you, and pray for those who spitefully use you.
> —MATTHEW 5:43–44

The Qur'an claims that Muhammad used spiritual assistance to win against overwhelming odds. Such commentary spurred the faithful on. The Lion, as Muhammad was sometimes called, and his followers were enticed with spoil. The quest for carnage quickened as their power grew. Those that died for the cause were promised heaven, while those that survived divided the spoils. Muhammad always publicly thanked Allah and gave him the glory. Today's terrorists view themselves as heroic visionaries restoring Islam to its former stature and glory.

It is commanded in the Qur'an, "Make war on those who believe not, even the People of the Book [Christians and Jews]. Make war on them until idolatry is no more and Allah's religion reigns supreme" (Sürah 9:29).

The followers of the Qur'an and its prophets are to leave no idol intact. They are duty bound to smash, burn and destroy them in the temple and in the sanctuary. A Christian church is considered a place of idolatry because in it Jesus is deified. Churches are to be destroyed. A Muslim works his way to heaven by partaking in these activities. He must do activity as prescribed by the god in the Qur'an and his puppet Muhammad. Satan has lied and told the Arab people that salvation is in their own hands.

He preaches no mediator between God and man. A Muslim is on his own, a church to himself. The deception is elementary: Remove the lifeline, and the people die.

The Bible tells an entirely different story: Only the blood of Jesus can save a person. "For the life of the flesh is in the blood, and I have given it to you upon the altar to make atonement for your souls; for it is the blood that makes atonement for the soul" (Lev. 17:11).

Jesus said:

> Abide in Me, and I in you. As the branch cannot bear fruit of itself, unless it abides in the vine, neither can you, unless you abide in Me. I am the vine, you are the branches. He who abides in Me, and I in him, bears much fruit; for without Me you can do nothing. If anyone does not abide in Me, he is cast out as a branch and is withered; and they gather them and throw them into the fire, and they are burned.
>
> —John 15:4–6

Satan has placed one of Islam's most sacred shrines, the Dome on the Rock, right where King Solomon's temple once stood on Mount Moriah. It was also on this Mount that Jesus is said to have been condemned to death. Satan has placed his shrine well. It will continue to be a source of strife for years to come.

Judgment day is coming. The folly of *jihad* can best be understood when it is viewed through the words of Jesus when He said, "Assuredly, I say to you, inasmuch as you did it to one of the least of these My brethren, you did it to Me" (Matt. 25:40).

10

Islam's Outward Face

Having a form of godliness...but they will progress
no further, for their folly will be manifest to all.
                                        —2 TIMOTHY 3:5, 9

The center of Islamic life is the mosque (*mosjid*). It
means place of prostration. The characteristics of
the mosques vary somewhat, but they have become
the predominant places of prayer and worship for Muslims.
Since there is no secular separation in Islam, the mosque
has become the heart, the very pulse of a Muslim's life.

The mosque, with its common distinguishing pillars,
originally began as a prototype of Muhammad's own house
and courtyard in Medina. It is where Muhammad first met
and communed with his ardent followers. The main part of
the house was used as a reverential sanctuary, while the
smaller private cubicles became shelters and meeting places
for the worshipers. The present-day mosques evolved
mostly from political and military circumstances.

The rather spatial arrangement of the mosque is orientated toward Mecca, the holy city of Islam. At every

moment, somewhere in the world, someone is prostrated toward Mecca. Curiously enough, Muhammad began his daily prayer of submission orientated toward the sacred shrine of the Kabah. After his transfer to Medina he changed the prayer direction to Jerusalem, but was spurned by the Jews for his imperfect understanding of the Scriptures. Angered, Muhammad changed the prayer direction (*quibla*) for the third time. This time it was changed once and for all to Mecca.

How Allah had Muhammad reveal such prayer directions and then change them is curious since the Qur'an reads, "...for no one ever can change the decrees of Allah" (Sürah 6:34).

The various dimensions and orientations were developed gradually. A familiar feature that Westerners notice first is the prominent high tower called the minaret. It is from this tower that the *muezzin* (Muslim crier) summons the faithful to prayer five times daily. The crier was used because Muhammad disliked the bells of Christian churches. Today this minaret has come to symbolize Islam and its unity.

The Taj Mahal is one of the most popular and prominent Muslim monuments, but only by Western standards. The most sacred shrine is the Kabah. It contains a small black oval rock or meteorite seven inches in diameter supposedly given to Muhammad by the angel Gabriel. Originally, the stone is said to have been white, but because of the sins of those that have touched it, over the centuries it turned black.[1]

Anyone entering the Kabah's stone cube (12 x 10 x 15 yards) must wear only white. Kabah comes from the Sanskrit word *gabha*. It is a word taken from the Indian Prakrit language that means the innermost sanctuary where a deity is to be installed. *Encyclopedia Islamia* names some of the images that were initially in the Kabah as Lat, Manat and Uzza. Many of these gods are still in vogue and worshiped in parts of the East.

Conflicting fables have the Kabah left over from Abraham's altar. It is claimed that he first instituted the rights of pilgrimage. Some say the Kabah was built by Abraham's firstborn son, Ishmael, and endued with supernatural powers. Still others say that Adam first built it exactly below a similar shrine in heaven. There is much lore and superstition connected with the shrine and its sacred stone that is always covered with a black veil.

While traveling in the East I met many people that worship stones. Some are taken from sacred rivers, and people actually attribute deity to them. Muslims also still persist in the worship of inanimate objects and use relics and fetishes to ward off *jinn* (devils).

Muhammad left this rock as an obvious concession to the prevalent animistic beliefs of the people as merchants had become angry when Muhammad abolished the idols. The pilgrims that had come to worship no longer brought their money. But Muhammad was politically gifted and a shrewd appraiser of others. He left the stone and modified the story to fit his own. He would never have won approval without some concessions and without claiming divine authorship.

So-called holy cities and spiritual shrines are closely guarded. No non-Muslim or infidel may enter into the city of Mecca under any circumstance. Such an intrusion is considered a grave sacrilege and can be punished by death. Near this city is Muhammad's burial place. It is considered a pure contact place between Allah and mankind. An infidel, they say, would defile such a place.

Mecca is derived from the Sanskrit word *makha*, which means "sacrifice (*yanja*) or sacrificial fire." It was in such fires that food and articles were offered to the gods. Medina comes from the Sanskrit word meaning land. Iran comes from the word *ira* (water), which was used in the purification rites of idols. These words were left from Sanskrit-speaking Indian *ksatriyas* (warriors) when they ruled the

100

land. Should we include all the Qur'anic words that find their roots in the idol-worshiping scriptures of the Far East, another book would be necessary. These Vedic spiritual remnants comprised the beliefs that Muhammad merged with his scant knowledge of Holy Scripture.

The cities mingle the sacred, public and private sectors of life. Next in importance to the highly decorated mosques are the crowded bazaars. They serve as a marketplace for all goods common to Islamic life. This entire scenario must be built near or around water, which is at a premium in the arid lands. It plays the most crucial role in everything from agriculture to the social aspects of baths and lavish gardens.

Given Muhammad's circumstance of living in the hot, arid desert and his passion for women, it is no wonder that he depicts heaven with cool, running streams set in an oasis setting. Much of the Qur'anic art depicts scenes made up of floral arrangements and abstracts from well-watered gardens of delight. This garden, laden with ripened fruit amid whispering streams and nymph-like virgin servants, is the common subject of expressions of paradise. The art can be breathtakingly beautiful with harmonious effects using the interplay of light. The architecture is replete with inlays and multicolored designs combined in stunning arrangements.

Islam borrowed its art and architecture from the cultures around it. Most of Islamic music, art, gardens and architecture can be traced to the East, primarily India. Most of the Islamic artistry was stolen during the many centuries of pillage and plunder. Much was obtained from converted courtiers. Like a major portion of Qur'anic ideas and ideals, Islam's outward appearance can be traced back to the ancient Vedic literatures (Sanskrit writings purported to be five thousand years old). A system of religion that thrives on conversions through intimidation, torture, killing and fire now lays claim to the plundered art and architecture as well.

11

Five Pillars and Five Articles

Muslims must accept five principal articles of faith:

1. They must believe in the final Day of Judgment.

2. They must accept twenty-eight prophets, Muhammad being the last and greatest.

3. They must believe that Allah and no other is the one true God.

4. They must maintain a belief in angels that do only Allah's will.

5. They must maintain an adherence to four inspired books:
   Torah of Moses (Pentateuch)
   Injil (Gospel of Jesus)

Zabur (Psalms of David)
Qur'an

The following five pillars are five requirements that every Muslim is expected to perform. It is part of the *Ibadat*, or commitment to the Qur'an's message. If one executes these parameters they believe heaven will be their home.

1. During the holy month of Ramadan, a kind of Lent, the Muslim must fast from all food and drink during the daytime. Even the swallowing of saliva is forbidden. Eating dates breaks the fast. It was during Ramadan that the Qur'an was said to have been brought down to the first heaven.

2. The second pillar demands from a Muslim that has the means a pilgrimage (*haji*) to Mecca once in their lifetime. This is considered the high point in the Muslim's lifetime. In the sacred arena a special dress (*ihram*) is worn. After an elaborate ceremony that lasts for days, they have their heads shaved. This symbol of worldly renunciation has been common throughout the East for thousands of years.

   The object of the pilgrimage is to worship before and circumambulate (*tawaf*) the Kabah. While doing so they try to touch or kiss the black stone inside. They go on to sacrifice an animal at Mina, which is the highlight of the *haji*. This is done to commemorate Abraham's willingness to sacrifice his only son. This is the second great festival of the Muslim calendar.

3. *Shahada*, or the public affirmation of faith, is

103

considered the most basic of pillars. Every Muslim must repeat, "There is no god but Allah, and Muhammad is his prophet." A serious Muslim must repeat this daily. The Shahada is emblazoned on the Saudi Arabian flag.

4. The Muslim is required to know the words and gestures to specific rituals that are done at specific times. Along with this he must pay a tax (*zakat*), which is similar to the Christian tithe.

5. The Muslim must pray to Allah five times a day. These prayers (*salat*) are recited at sunrise, at noon, in the afternoon, at sunset and in the evening. Before prayer one must wash (*wadu*). *Salat* begins in the standing position. Bows are made from the waist (*ruku*), and then to the floor. The head must touch the ground (*sujud*). Verses from the Qur'an are recited on the Friday *salat*, and the congregation is summoned from the minaret.

12

Sufism

> But even if our gospel is veiled, it is veiled to those
> who are perishing, whose minds the god of this age
> has blinded, who do not believe, lest the light of the
> gospel of the glory of Christ, who is the image of
> God, should shine on them.
>
> —2 CORINTHIANS 4:3–4

Islam relegates love to a tenth class status, but the desire of an intimate loving relationship with an absolute supreme being has endured. Altruism in Islam has been quietly absorbed into the mainstream of everyday life. Rising out of the cold, rigid legalism of Islam comes this aberration, this undeniable ferment called Sufism (*tasawwuf*). This variety of mysticism was born because the radical orthodoxy denied personal communion with God.

This enduring human ardor is the source of most of the original literature, music or emotion found in Islam. The Sufi (wool wearer) follows a path that is very similar to the master/disciple relationship found in the Far East.

God created mankind in His own image and likeness

(Gen. 1:26). No matter how this innate nature is suppressed, denied or bound, it must find expression. Sufism has managed to carve out a significant niche within mainstream Islam as an alternative to the submission based on fear and prohibition that characterizes the official religion.

Sufism emphasizes a supernatural search for the life force and attributes of a beloved God. It amplifies a personal relationship and devotion to Allah rather than the callous and invented mandates of the Qur'an. Like the idol worshipers of the Far East, Sufis believe in reincarnation. Trying to fill a desperate void, they search for Brahman, which is a state where the soul (*atman*) merges with ultimate reality.

A small atom can find expression when suppressed by divulging the inherent life of its underlying energy in an explosive demonstration. Jesus, the force behind all life, was crucified on Calvary and buried. When Satan tried to repress the promised Savior, eternal life burst out of death. The Qur'an will never extinguish this force.

Considered oddities and tolerated as an embarrassment, the Sufis hold on to the belief that God will reveal Himself to the ardent seeker. The Bible says He will. These monks have minimal influence and hold no political power in Islam. The world is hardly aware of their existence, but Sufism presents a great hope of true revival. For it is written, "But from there you will seek the LORD your God, and you will find Him if you seek Him with all your heart and with all your soul" (Deut. 4:29).

Satan controls the Islamic countries by his terror and confusion, but he cannot control the realm of God's Spirit. He cannot crush the human sentiment for love. It is naturally inherent in everyone. All who have an honest heart will eventually respond to love.

The deep rift between the legalistic fundamentalists and the Sufis began early on. The Sufis were considered weak, purely sentimental and undisciplined. This rift was evident in the life of Husayn ibn Mansur al-Hallaj, an ecstatic Sufi mystic who openly sought love of God. In the year A.D. 922, he was charged with blasphemy. He had surrendered his life to Jesus Christ and accepted Him as his Master. He said it was on the basis of Scripture, especially the verse where Jesus proclaims, "I am…the truth" (John 14:6).

In response the legalists claimed that the truth is God, but that Jesus was not the truth, hence not God. Husayn was tried, but he would not recant his belief. He was publicly scourged and crucified. Tremendous persecution followed, but Sufism survived. Sufis consider Husayn ibn Mansur al-Hallaj a holy martyr and a saint whose only crime was to publicize the deepest truth.

Nevertheless, other Islamic poets, storytellers and critics have from time to time stepped forward in the face of death. Their tears surfaced above the medieval legalism that supported the early rulers. Abu Said ibn Abi Khayr (A.D. 1049), an abbot of a large Sufi monastery, propagated an almost open hostility toward the cold, rigid *ulama* (law). He encouraged love of God, spiritual dance, song and joy. He regarded the Islamic law as unadulterated bondage. He accurately referred to the Kabah as a "house of stone."[1]

Other Sufis have risen through the system of death and found the love they sought. Their unending cries can be heard above the Islamic drone of verses that emanates from the minarets.

A segment yearns for the good things, and they claim that only the reprehensible remains.[2] Sufis relate to the verse, "…ye are poor unto Allah and Allah, he is rich, the object of all praise" (Sürah 47:38).

With the decline of religious fervor in the eighteenth and nineteenth centuries, converts besieged Sufism. The zeal of persecution abated about this time, and every madman and pervert became a Sufi. Soon, every uncommon mental condition was attributed to renunciation of the world and sainthood.

All in all, Sufism can be credited with keeping a door open to the love of God and deep religious feeling. It provides color in an otherwise banal religion of bondage and death. The Sufis carry on and salvage the affairs of the heart. They write reflective poems and allegories that expose the thirsty Islamic soul. They have displayed an extraordinary wit and handed down a great story-telling heritage. They are the part of Islam that announces hope.

Many different Sufi orders, or brotherhoods, exist. Each has its own head or designated saint, and each saint has his own religious program. They are called *shaykhs*, *pirs*, *rahbars* or *muquaddams*. Those that live communally are called *shagrids* or *murids*. When a *murid* reaches spiritual maturation, he is sent by the *shaykh* to preach and spread the brotherhood's particular message throughout the countryside. Some Sufis venerate Muhammad to the level of an incarnation. They call him the Light of lights.

The *shaykh* also chooses and initiates a successor, or *khalifah*. Each order has its own unique spiritual meditation, or *dhikr*. It is usually comprised of words chanted over and over, often on beads, as an aid to remembering Allah.

The Bible warns of such futile attempts at reaching God: "But when you pray, do not use vain repetitions as the heathen do. For they think they will be heard for their many words" (Matt. 6:7).

One brotherhood, quite recognizable in the West, is the cult of the whirling dervish, from *darvash* (poor). This idiosyncratic spiritual deportment arose within the Melevi order of Turkey and was founded by the mystic poet Halal al-Din al-Rumi. Dervishes whirl, howl and bark in spiritual trances and claim they enter the cosmic flow of the universe.

Sufism is a unique blend of an inner plea for God's love and Eastern mysticism. The Sufi thrives on *rasas* (spiritual tastes) that are developed through techniques such as

reciting mantras (words and chants designed to invite spiritual moods or gods) or dance. Another similarity to
Eastern mysticism is the guru-disciple type of relationship
between the saint and the aspirant. Astrology, soothsaying,
hypnotic rituals, chanting, divination and a reverence for
possession by long-departed spiritual masters are
paramount objectives. For the most part, Sufism is a sad
confusion for those that truly seek God. In most cases it is
nothing more than man's vain attempt to ascend the mys-
tical states through ancient satanic sciences.

Solomon declared ages ago:

> That which has been is what will be, that which is
> done is what will be done, and there is nothing new
> under the sun. Is there anything of which it may be
> said, "See, this is new"? It has already been in ancient
> times before us.
>
> —ECCLESIASTES 1:9–10

In a poetic rendition the dervish is given high accolades.
He is said to spread the secrets of the universe without seeking a reward and to give away entire kingdoms in a breath.
But Sufis will eventually find the spiritual kingdoms and
heavenly realms of bliss to be satanic counterfeits. Whether
advocating obvious demise or using the lure of splendor,
these spiritual kingdoms are extremely dangerous. The
Bible says, "For we do not wrestle against flesh and blood,
but against principalities, against powers, against the rulers
of the darkness of this age, against spiritual hosts of wickedness in the heavenly places" (Eph. 6:12).

By attaining to these heavenly places, a Sufi can develop
mystic powers much like an Eastern yogi. They seek to attain
to a high level of excellence called *barakah*. Seekers try to
associate with such persons to learn secrets or to gain a benefit. In a sort of medieval sense, the Sufis' search can be

compared to the sixties' pursuit after gurus and masters in order to find enlightenment or power. It is a mysterious world that is hidden in the darker side of reality. It is a common ploy used by Satan. He offers age-old mysteries and power to lure a soul. He even tried to tempt Jesus once with the whole world. (See Matthew 4:8–10.)

It is purported that men who perfect these powers can perform miracles (*karamat*). The faithful seek them and visit their tombs when they die for benefits. A Sufi is not supposed to publicly display these powers.

The path (*tariqah*) is lined with rules (*shariah*) that have developed through years of repetitious happenstance. Knowledge of this path is handed down in disciplic succession in an unbroken chain. Again, this parallels the Eastern idolaters system of *parampara* (disciplic succession). The highest power attainable is called *qutb*, where one becomes one with the pole or pivot of the universe. It is equal to a lower level of Eastern mysticism.

Since the Muslim claims to be an extension of the prophets and to adhere to their teachings, the Sufi would do well to heed the prophet's words:

> Stand now with your enchantments and the multitude of your sorceries, in which you have labored from your youth—perhaps you will be able to profit, perhaps you will prevail. You are wearied in the multitude of your counsels; let now the astrologers, the stargazers, and the monthly prognosticators stand up and save you from what shall come upon you. Behold, they shall be as stubble, the fire shall burn them; they shall not deliver themselves from the power of the flame.
>
> —Isaiah 47:12–14

13

Islamic Law and Divisions

Do not think that I came to destroy the Law or the Prophets. I did not come to destroy but to fulfill.
—Matthew 5:17

In Islam it is Muhammad's rendition of reality that fulfills the law. Jesus is recognized, but virtually overlooked. Muhammad said, "He who obeys me obeys Allah. He who does not obey me does not obey Allah."

Although there is no clergy in Islam, there is a professional class called *ulama*, which literally means learned man. These men guard the orthodoxy. This means the religious beliefs and also the legislation of that which the West would call civil law.

The controlling *ulama* wield extensive and all-inclusive power. They regulate both the interpretation of the law as well as its underlying theology. They teach in institutions of higher learning called *madrasanas*. They also preserve and defend against what they call the eroding effects of the Western world and guard against any modernist movement within Islam itself.

Laws are for Muslims only. In an Islamic country, a non-Muslim can never have any authority over a Muslim. A Christian cannot testify in a court case against a Muslim because the Qur'an forbids the testimony of an infidel. Thus, property is easily seized, church land taken away and any civil claim brought against a Muslim by a non-Muslim cast out.

Not only does Islam remove the hope of eternal life in Jesus, but also its constricting tentacles bind its followers in everyday life. There is no separation of church and state. Islamic doctrine is Islamic law. Allah's word, as interpreted by Muhammad, is the government, economy, religion and the social life of every Muslim.

Uncompromisingly strict laws that bind the Muslim by fear of physical punishment or death uphold morality. Thieves can have their hands cut off. Sin is restricted with brutality. Stoning punishes adultery. Everything opposed to Allah's laws leads to death. Some of the laws were taken from the Old Testament, while Muhammad contrived most the rest.

Unlike Christianity, the major motivational factor in Islam is not love, but fear. Graphic depictions of Allah's terrors on judgment day, tortures and sadistic rituals in hellish places are taught as destinations for those that live outside of the Qur'an's unbending will. Anyone that does not surrender to Muhammad's interpretation is to suffer terror in this life and in the afterlife.

The Qur'an states:

> There they shall neither taste refreshment nor any drink save boiling water and decaying filth, they will drink molten metal, a fitting recompense. Hell will lie in ambush, a home for transgressors.
> —SŪRAH 78:21–26

Know they not that for those who oppose Allah and His apostle is the fire of Hell? Wherein they shall dwell. That is the supreme disgrace.

—SŪRAH 9:63

The inhabitants of paradise will call to the inhabitants of the fire; we have found what our lord promised us as true. Yes! They will say. And then a herald shall proclaim among them: Allah's curse is on the evildoers who bar from Allah's way, desiring to make it crooked, disbelieving in the world to come.

—SŪRAH 7:44–45

There is a correlation here with biblical Christianity in that there is a fiery, godless hell for miscreants. The parallel ceases there. The Muslim is asked to surrender without any tenderness or love, without Jesus. All individuality is taken away and merged into the supreme will of the Qur'an. It demands sovereignty and submission according to its ordinance. This is not so strange since Satan, who is responsible for this scriptural distortion, could never love anyone. A Muslim is simply robbed and left to a life without Jesus, who is love and God.

The Bible tells us, "He has delivered us from the power of darkness and conveyed us into the kingdom of the Son of His love, in whom we have redemption through His blood, the forgiveness of sins" (Col. 1:13–14).

And old Islamic legend reveals the uncompromising demands on a person's individuality: One fine day a young man in search of truth knocked on Allah's mighty door. "Who are you?" Allah demanded. "It is I," replied the inquisitive young man meekly. The stern voice from inside the huge door spoke again: "Go," it said; "in my house there is no room for you and me." The young man withdrew sheepishly. This answer left him dumbfounded. He ventured into the desert where he prayed and fasted for a long time.

Much time passed in deep meditation, and then once again the young man traveled to Allah's door. Finding himself before the great door, the young man confidently knocked again. "Who are you?" the voice inside boomed. "I am you," the young believer replied. The door opened.

The young man had reached the goal of *fana*, or the complete extinction of the self. *Fana* means that one is to turn from everything in the world, those in the world and themselves. All must come under the subservience of the Qur'an's instructions. *Fana* leads to *baqa*, or the enduring condition of being bound forever. A terrorist on a suicide mission is the best example of one who has reached the platform of *fana*. He has given himself up as dictated in the Qur'an.

Jesus created us, not to take away our individuality, but through love to share it with us. A born-again Christian becomes a child of the King and His heir. God will share eternity with us!

> The Spirit Himself bears witness with our spirit that we
> are children of God, and if children then heirs—heirs
> of God and joint heirs with Christ, if indeed we suffer
> with Him, that we may also be glorified together.
> —ROMANS 8:16–17

Islam does contain human elements, for there are differing opinions and different schools with each having its own specific point of view. Every faction guards its own chains of authenticity. There are acute sects and divisions, but the most pronounced and visible are the Sunnis and the Shiites. They have been participants in the recent lengthy war between Iraq and Iran. Iraq is a Sunni state while Iran is Shiite. The Shiites are the more fiercely zealous of the two, as can be attested to by the radical policies of the imams in Iran.

The divisions began immediately after Muhammad's death for he named no successor and died without a male offspring. A dispute began concerning caliphal succession, and early on the Sunnis dominated. Religious leaders elect this highest-ranking religious leader. The first caliph was known as Rashidan (rightly guided). The decision to award the caliphate went to Abu Bakr, Muhammad's father-in-law. The Sunnis chose the first four caliphs. There followed many curses, deaths and poisonings.

The Shiites (*Shiat Ali*) are the followers of what they say is Muhammad's direct family line. The Shiites rejected the first caliphs. Their belief is that Muhammad chose Ali as the recipient of some special esoteric understanding. This understanding was passed down from father to son. They say that no one else is capable of understanding it. It is believed that a special divine light was fully incarnate in Ali and transferred upon death to the next worthy recipient.

The spiritual leaders in this line are called the imams. These rulers, such as the late Ayatollah Khomeini, are considered virtually infallible and are largely responsible for the current upheavals of *jihad*. Honor in Islam is reserved for these imams, the religious hierarchy in general, famous poets and the tombs of saints.

The Sunnis were responsible for a great massacre of Shiites that occurred in the year A.D. 680. Ali's son Hussain and seventy-two relatives were killed by the Sunnis. Ali was the first Shiite and was considered to have assumed Muhammad's mantle. This division has continued to this very day. The Shiites are uncompromising and serve the Qur'an with great passion. They have their own sects of suicidal assassins and literally believe that martyrdom is the quickest way to heaven.

The Shiite Ashura festival has its origin in the martyrdom of Imam Husyan on the field of Karbala. On this day of mourning black flags are flown. Men beat themselves on the back with small knives suspended on chains. They flip them over their heads and cut themselves deeply as the bloody procession intensifies. This, they say, pleases Allah and shows their dedication.

The human element fosters more complications. There are various groups that recognize different imams. The laws that govern these various groups differ little in that they are taken from the Qur'an and its supplements. There are many extensions to the Qur'an that are sanctioned, but suspect. Twelver Schism is the official religion of Iran for the last five to six hundred years. They recognize twelve imams. Another group is called Seveners or Ismalis. They are the most radical and murderous fundamentalists.

There is a splinter group familiar to the West called the Bahai or Bahaiism. In 1847 a man named Mizra Hussayn Ali called himself the glory of Allah (*Bahau Allah*). His grand spiritual concept was to unite the three great religions of Judaism, Christianity and Islam.

While Muhammad was still alive, he was the sole infallible law. After Muhammad died, the attention of his followers turned to facts about his life. These facts were recorded as sayings of Muhammad written in books called the Hadiths and the Sunnas.

The Hadiths are a collection of third-century books now considered second in authority to the Qur'an. They are called the Six Sahih Books and were compiled when spiritual leaders sifted through bad prophetic judgments. The books are both historical and controversial. They mirror the medieval Muslim mentality. These books contain *sunnas* (rules or commands) given by Muhammad. Recently, some schools have rejected these appendages in favor of the Qur'an. The sects differ in that they stress different parts of these texts.

Al-Shafii, who died in A.D. 820, worked out the majority of the rules of law. His work has won general acceptance throughout Islam. His theory of *usul al-fiqh* (roots or sources of law) puts forth four *usul*, which stand in order of rank. First, and without equal, is the Qur'an. Second is the Sunnah, which is the prophet's direct commands, translated in valid Hadith. It is the supplement, but never independent of the Qur'an. Third, if an answer is not available in the first two, a lawyer (*faqih*) may turn to the community for a consensus (*ijma*). The basis for this shred of democracy is a principle in the Hadith that states that no Muslim community could ever agree in error. The fourth is reason (*qiyas*). It is only to be used with great caution and only when the other three methods have failed.

Law has two duties: first, to their god (*Ibadat*), and second, to the people (*Muamalat*). Both sets of duties are instituted by the divine decree through the Qur'an. It is said to be an eternal pattern ordained for the universe. This path is all-inclusive for mankind and to be extended through *jihad*.

14

Jesus, a Mere Man?

God was manifested in the flesh, justified in the Spirit, seen by angels, preached among the Gentiles, believed on in the world, received up into glory.

—1 TIMOTHY 3:16

The Bible is clear that salvation in Jesus the Messiah is available for all people, both Jews and Gentiles of all nations. During Jesus' earthly and personal ministry He first instructed His disciples to go only to the Israelites. But after His atoning death on the cross, He then told His disciples, "You shall be witnesses to Me in Jerusalem, and in all Judea and Samaria, and to the end of the earth" (Acts 1:8). He also told them, "Go…and make disciples of all the nations" (Matt. 28:19).

Jesus Himself confirmed the universal nature of His mission when He declared these words: "I am the light of the world. He who follows Me shall not walk in darkness, but have the light of life" (John 8:12). While Islam accepts Jesus as a prophet, they abhor the belief that He was God. One of the first things a Muslim comes to know about the

Christian religion is the belief that God had a wife who conceived for Him a son named Jesus. They ask, "How can He have a son when He has no consort?" The Qur'an states, "Christ the son of Mary was no more than an Apostle; many were the Apostles that passed away before him" (Sürah 5:75). The Islamic claim that Jesus was no more than a Prophet undermines all scriptural integrity.

Jesus' birth as the Messiah was prophesied in Scripture. Muhammad's birth as the so-called Seal of the Prophets was not. There were hundred of prophecies concerning Jesus, all of which came true in Him. Who prophesied the birth of Muhammad as a true prophet of God? No one, except Muhammad. Throughout the Qur'an, Muhammad refutes that Jesus was the Son of God:

> Christ Jesus the son of Mary was (no more than) an Apostle of God, and His Word, which He bestowed on Mary, and a Spirit proceeding from Him.
> —Sürah 4:171

> Christ the son of Mary was no more than an Apostle; many were the Apostles that passed away before him. His mother was a woman of truth. They had both to eat their (daily) food. See how Allah doth make His Signs clear to them; yet see in what ways they are deluded away from the truth!
> —Sürah 5:75

> To Him is due the primal origin of the heavens and the earth: how can He have a son when He hath no consort? He created all things, and He hath full knowledge of all things.
> —Sürah 6:101

> The Jews call Uzair [Ezra] a son of God, and the Christians call Christ the son of God. That is a saying

119

from their mouths; (in this) they but imitate what the Unbelievers of old used to say.

—SÜRAH 9:30

They [the Christians] say, "God hath begotten a son!" Glory be to Him! He is Self-Sufficient! His are all things in the heavens and on earth! No warrant [authority] have ye for this! Say ye about God what ye know not? Say: "Those who invent a lie against God will never prosper." A little enjoyment in this world!—and, then, to Us will be their return. Then shall We make them taste the severest Penalty for their blasphemies.

—SÜRAH 10:68–70

Praise be to Allah Who begets no son.

—SÜRAH 17:111

They say: "(God) Most Gracious has begotten a son!" Indeed ye have put forth a thing most monstrous! As if the skies are ready to burst, the earth to split asunder, and the mountains to fall down in utter ruin, that they should invoke a son for (God) Most Gracious. For it is not consonant with the majesty of (God) Most Gracious that He should beget a son.

—SÜRAH 19:88–92

No son has He [Allah] begotten.

—SÜRAH 25:2

Is it not that they say, from their own invention, "God has begotten children"? But they are liars!

—SÜRAH 37:151–152

When (Jesus) the son of Mary is held up as an example, behold, thy people raise a clamor thereat (in ridicule)! And they say, "Are Our gods best, or He?"

> This they set forth to thee, only by way of disputation:
> yea, they are a contentious people. He was no more
> than a servant: We granted Our favor to him, and We
> made him an example to the Children of Israel.
> —SŪRAH 43:57–59

It was Muhammad's self-proclaimed mission to warn those who say, "God has taken to Himself a son." Yet, almost every prophet has testified of the Messiah's Sonship:

> For unto us a Child is born, unto us a Son is given.
> —ISAIAH 9:6

> He will be great, and will be called the Son of the
> Highest...The Holy Spirit will come upon you, and
> the power of the Highest will overshadow you; there-
> fore, also, that Holy One who is to be born will be
> called the Son of God.
> —LUKE 1:32, 35

John the Baptist bore record that Jesus was the Son of God (John 1:32–34). God Himself testified twice of Jesus: "This is My beloved Son, in whom I am well pleased" (Matt. 3:17; 17:5; Mark 1:11; 9:7; Luke 3:22; 9:35). Mark also testified in his Gospel, ""Jesus Christ, the Son of God" (Mark 1:1).

Even the unclean spirits recognized that Jesus was the Son of God: "And suddenly they cried out, saying, 'What have we to do with You, Jesus, You Son of God? Have You come here to torment us before the time?'" (Matt. 8:29).

To casual observers and lifeless Christians, Muhammad's claim of God having no Son in Jesus does not seem to be so very damaging. After all, they think, he did acknowledge that Jesus was a prophet, a Messenger of God. If Muhammad had stated that Jesus was not a prophet, but the Messiah, then his entire message of the Qur'an would have been of non-effect, and those he preached to would have become Christians. A statement that Jesus was God would have precluded their even listening to his message. Further, we can't fail to understand that Muhammad had to include Jesus within his teachings if he was to be more convincing concerning his own authority. It is easier to deceive if you pretend to build on some aspect of truth. Deception always starts with truth but ends in a lie.

And quite contrary to the message of love that Jesus preached, Muhammad had little love to lose when he stated, "Take not friends from their ranks [the unbelievers] until they flee in the way of Allah from what is forbidden. But if they turn renegades, seize them and slay them wherever ye find them" (Sürah 4:89). "Slay the unbelievers wherever you find them, and take them, and confine them, and lie in wait for them at every place of ambush" (Sürah 9:5). "When you meet the unbelievers, smite their necks, then, when you have made wide slaughter among them, tie fast the bonds; then set them free, either by grace or ransom, till the war lays down its loads" (Sürah 47:5).

Muhammad didn't want to sit around and philosophize the differing points of view of Jesus the Son of God, Jesus not the Son of God. He forced the issue with the sword and made up verses to kill all who worshiped Jesus. But the Lord asks us to follow Him and to trust in Him; He will repay the evildoers.

> Beloved, do not avenge yourselves, but rather give place to wrath; for it is written, "Vengeance is Mine, I will repay," says the Lord. Therefore "if your enemy is hungry, feed him; if he is thirsty, give him a drink; for in so doing you will heap coals of fire on his head." Do not be overcome by evil, but overcome evil with good.
> —ROMANS 12:19–21

Throughout the Qur'an, Muhammad attempts to undercut the role of Christ Jesus as Savior and downgrade Jesus to a mere man. He tries to negate that the Lamb of God bore our sins and made intercession for transgressors. "Come, the Apostle of Allah [meaning Muhammad] will pray for your forgiveness" (Sürah 63:5).

Muhammad denies that Jesus was ever crucified: "They killed him not, nor crucified him, but so it was made to appear to them" (Sürah 4:157). Central to Christianity is the doctrine of salvation through the atonement on the cross for our sins. Jesus reconciled us to the Father that we might receive forgiveness and grace. By resisting temptation all the way to Calvary, Jesus was victorious over the Satan. He brought us the gift of life and made a way through the insidious evil in the world. He simply says, "Come, follow Me."

Jesus made a way for us to get back to our God. To say that Jesus was just a mortal is a lie. To say that He was not the Son of God is a lie. To say that He did not die for our sins is a lie.

> Who is a liar but he who denies that Jesus is the Christ? He is antichrist who denies the Father and the Son. Whosoever denies the Son does not have the Father either; he who acknowledges the Son has the Father also.
>
> —1 JOHN 2:22–23

> By this you know the Spirit of God: Every spirit that confesses that Jesus Christ has come in the flesh is of God, and every spirit that does not confess that Jesus Christ has come in the flesh is not of God. And this is the spirit of the Antichrist, which you have heard was coming, and is now already in the world.
>
> —1 JOHN 4:2–3

> For many deceivers have gone out into the world who do not confess Jesus Christ as coming in the flesh.

Jesus vs. Jihad

This is a deceiver and an antichrist.

—2 John 7

The discerning reader should readily see that Muhammad tried to make Jesus' life of null effect for sinners. True, Muhammad has been just one of many who have tried to discredit the Savior.

Perhaps the greatest obstacle keeping Muslims from accepting the truth of the New Testament is the Crucifixion. They adamantly refuse to accept that Jesus died on the cross, and they insist the whole story is a hoax to deceive Christians. Many Muslims further claim this is why the Qur'an was revealed. It came to correct this false teaching about Jesus dying on the cross. Muhammad laid claim to being the final prophet and the bearer of the final revelation for mankind. The Qur'an and its implications deny the prophecies and deity of Jesus. Islam attempts to make Jesus a liar.

While Jesus ministered on earth, He was a homeless vagabond with no place to lay His head. He had no home, wife, children or livelihood. At age thirty-three, He was unceremoniously crucified on a wooden cross. He had been charged with blasphemy and awarded a death reserved for the worst of criminals. This Wanderer has been and still is the subject of endless debates. No other name springs forth from the pages of history with more controversy than does the wonderful name of Jesus.

Two thousand years have elapsed since Jesus traveled the dusty roads of the Middle East. Since His return to heaven, wars have been waged, and countries have been founded, divided and destroyed because of the principles and claims He presented. Everyone tries to categorize Him. Some religions make Him another spoke on the greater wheel of many masters. Communism unapologetically denies Him. The humanist makes Him relative to other men, and Islam

124

has set out to blatantly destroy His deity. But Jesus is the very heart of God displayed. Jesus is God in the flesh. He came out of His infinite love to atone for our sins.

> For in Him [Jesus] dwells all the fullness of the Godhead bodily; and you are complete in Him, who is the head of all principality and power.
> —Colossians 2:9

Jesus suffered the agony of the lost and fallen souls incapable of saving themselves. He came with love, not force. He died for all men. He died for me. He died for the misguided Muslim. He died for Osama bin Laden. Islam denies this saving power and His purpose. In the Qur'an, Jesus is portrayed as a mere man.

Today we find most of history is divided into B.C. and A.D, before Christ and after Christ. This is not an extraordinary marvel, nor is it happenstance. We can find deep within the Eastern Vedic scriptures a weapon Satan claims to be his own. This weapon is called *chakra kala*, or time. The four-armed form, commonly seen in Eastern depictions of the primeval Hindu god Vishnu (Krishna), whirls this weapon of time around the index finger of one of his arms. It comes as no major surprise that Jesus rent time in two with His gift of eternal life. For it is written, "He who sins is of the devil, for the devil has sinned from the beginning. For this purpose the Son of God was manifested, that He might destroy the works of the devil" (1 John 3:8).

Jesus claimed to be God Himself (Luke 22:70). If Jesus is God, then Islam is just another clever product of the wicked genius of Satan. If Jesus is God, then a wonderful gate has been opened through which mankind can enter and find safety from Islam and other such meaningless webs of deceit.

The apostles accompanied Jesus throughout His public ministry. They loved and revered Him. They believed that

125

they had found the promised Messiah of the Old Testament. They believed that Jesus would release them from the oppressive rulers of the day. In the three years that they walked with Him they witnessed marvels and manifold miracles. He opened blind eyes, made the lame walk and raised the dead. The Bible tells us that so many miracles were performed that it would be impossible to record them all.

After witnessing such marvelous events, the apostles were prepared to follow Jesus anywhere and do anything He asked. They believed that He would soon reveal His true identity and the world would see the glory of the King of kings. Together they would rise and crush the tyrannical godless empire that enslaved them.

The apostles were sold out. They had left their livelihoods, families and friends to commune with Jesus. We can only imagine the crushing psychological blow that assailed their minds when the scenario of the Crucifixion unfolded. They must have watched in horror as Jesus was charged with being a despicable criminal and a blasphemer. They watched as He was scourged, crowned with thorns, spat upon, mocked and finally nailed to the gruesome cross. It was a most hideous death reserved for only the worst of offenders. This very death Islam denies.

When the apostles viewed the mangled, bloody body as it hung lifeless on the cross, they had to have been utterly shaken. It must have seemed as if life had dealt them a most irreparably cruel blow. It had to have simply pulverized their grasp on reality. They might even have asked, "What has happened to our beloved Master?" We might say in our modern vernacular that they had their minds blown.

The apostles were terrified at the events they had witnessed. Now they were afraid for their own lives as they scurried off to the hills where they were left with the awesome task of reconstructing their reeling minds. How could they rationalize this overwhelming dilemma? To whom would they turn?

Gone was the miracle worker. Gone was the Jesus they so loved. Gone was their King. In His place lay a slain leader, a bloodied and lifeless corpse. Life as they had come to know it had come to an end. Their lives were shattered. They had become victims of the cruelest hoax of all time—or had they?

Under ordinary circumstances, many a person could be expected to sag under the strain of such a psychological blow. Some might even be expected to "lose it" altogether. At the very least, the apostles could be expected to be seriously divided in their evaluations and opinions. They might be expected to scatter to the four winds. Quite possibly the ones with stronger constitutions might have made their way home and healed slowly.

Curiously, we find here history's most triumphant moment. After three days in the tomb, Jesus rose from the dead and returned to them. What happened was a phenomenon unparalleled in history. Jesus had conquered death! Jesus had conquered Satan and everything he could throw at Him. Subsequently, all the apostles, save for John, suffered martyrs' deaths. They died as they preached a risen Christ!

The apostles knew that as they preached they were in danger of losing their lives. They are not unlike the Christians today who are converted in Islamic nations. They know they might die, but the price for eternal life is worth the price of physical death. Death may have been plausible for perhaps one or two of the apostles. Perhaps a few would be deluded by their ordeal, gone mad in the aftermath and decided to create a facade. They might have conspired to save face and create their own reality. After all, they had left all things for Jesus. Maybe they would have felt they had nothing left to lose. Perhaps what was left of their pride would have overwhelmed them to the point of sheer delusion. But for all the apostles to return in total agreement, and then to punctuate their beliefs with a martyr's death, is not at all consistent with human nature.

Peter, as he preached the message of salvation in Jesus' name, was apprehended by the authorities of the day. When threatened with crucifixion he asked to be crucified upside down. He said he felt unworthy to be crucified right side up as was his Master. This was the same cowardly Peter who had denied Jesus three times in order to save his own hide (John 18:17–27). His newfound boldness is a direct result of having seen Jesus again and of having received the Holy Spirit Jesus promised. Peter saw a risen Christ!

Peter wrote, "For we did not follow cunningly devised fables when we made known to you the power of the coming of our Lord Jesus Christ, but were eyewitnesses to His majesty" (2 Pet. 1:16).

The other apostles had the same indisputable attitudes, preached the same gospel and met similar fates. They died from stoning, crucifixions, the sword and beheading. Only John, who miraculously survived being boiled alive in oil, died a natural death. The Lord still had a work for him. He had to write the Book of Revelation.

For such a flock to reassemble and have these unlikely events transpire is nothing short of incredible. To have so many disciples go willingly to their deaths points to an exceptional love. It points toward the absolute. They gave up life itself for Jesus. In light of the extraordinary sequence of events, it is not sound judgment to believe that all the early Christians were part of some conspiracy to let lions chew on them. They knew something. They had seen Jesus!

Paul, the apostle to the Gentiles, had been a zealous Pharisee before he met Jesus on the Damascus Road. He was highly educated and held a position of the highest esteem. He was in charge of killing the Christians, yet after his encounter with the Lord, he too repented and gave up his life to serve Him.

Paul eventually wrote, "But what things were gain to me, these things I have counted loss for Christ. Yet indeed I also count all things loss for the excellence of the knowledge of Christ Jesus my Lord, for whom I have suffered the loss of all things, and count them as rubbish, that I may win Christ" (Phil. 3:7–8). He also wrote, "For to me, to live is Christ, and to die is gain" (Phil. 1:21).

Eyewitnesses to Jesus' resurrection included apostles, disciples, Roman soldiers, friends and His own mother. There were many eyewitness accounts (Matt. 28; Mark 16; Luke 24; John 20; 21; Acts 1). There was a risen Christ. There is no other feasible explanation.

We might entertain the notion that men might die for a lie. After all, many have done so before. People not in touch with reality can be easily deceived. But not many men die for lies that they know are lies. Some men have died for lies that they thought to be true. If the Resurrection did not take place, the apostles knew it, for they watched Jesus die on the cross. There was no mistake on their part. They either saw a resurrected Jesus or they did not. For this number of men to have died the kind of brutal deaths for a lie is not at all likely.[1]

Other eyewitness accounts were also written and documented by other apostles. They themselves at first doubted that Jesus had risen. Thomas had to put his hands into Jesus' wounds before he believed. "Then He [Jesus] said to Thomas, 'Reach your finger here, and look at My hands; and reach your hand here, and put it into My side. Do not be unbelieving, but believing.' And Thomas answered and said to Him, 'My Lord and my God!'" (John 20:27–28).

An interesting proposition indeed, an account so fascinating it is worthy of anyone's contemplation. Were it all to end there, perhaps we would relegate it to one of life's unsolved mysteries. But fortunately, this was just the beginning.

Upon closer scrutiny, the Bible reveals to us a scenario aside from the miracles, the martyrdom of the apostles, apart from Jesus' own claim, apart from the virgin birth and apart from the Resurrection. The depth within its pages is unending, and the resplendence that adorns its corridors of intrigue befits only God Himself. It tells a story that is unalterable and undeniable.

> For the word of God is living and powerful, and sharper than any two-edged sword, piercing even to the division of soul and spirit, and of joints and marrow, and is a discerner of the thoughts and intents of the heart.
>
> —HEBREWS 4:12

This Word is all-inclusive. It is given a place that is unique by God Himself: "You have magnified Your word above all Your name" (Ps. 138:2). We have this incredible Word that is filled with unending revelations and ultimate disclosures. Islam accepts the Bible as God's Word, but claims it is distorted and incomplete. But no one can successfully tamper with or distort God's Word.

> For assuredly, I say to you, till heaven and earth pass away, one jot or one tittle will by no means pass from the law till all is fulfilled.
>
> —MATTHEW 5:18

When the Bible was first being written, mankind was not as yet civilized as we now term civilization. It was not written by one man in a cave somewhere suffering from an incredible, overly vivid futuristic imagination, but it was written piecemeal by forty different authors over a period of sixteen hundred years.

Within the pages of the Old Testament there are over three hundred prophecies concerning the approaching life of Jesus. There are sixty major prophecies and two hundred seventy ramifications, the last one of which was made four hundred years before Jesus' incarnation. These prophecies were not made up after His birth. This is well documented in the Greek Septuagint Scriptures, translated 150–250 B.C.

Most of these authors did not know one another. There was no collaboration. There could have been no collusion. The apostles who were eyewitnesses to His life, death and resurrection backed all these books. Such affairs simply could not have taken place at random. It is humanly impossible to contrive such a format in terms of time, capacity and the era in which they happened, much less duplicate its execution.

Unity under the most diverse of circumstances attests to the Bible's divine authorship. It was written across two continents in dungeons, tents, deserts and palaces—in times of danger and in times of joy. The writers were kings, judges, priests, prophets, patriarchs, prime ministers, herdsmen, scribes, soldiers, physicians and fishermen. Yet the Bible portrays and displays a unity beyond question. It speaks of God and the Redeemer He would send. It goes on to the fulfillment of that promise. It has one plan of salvation and one doctrine. Every promise and every prophecy have come to pass in the life of Jesus. The Bible boasts a superhuman character that lives on through the ages in its pages. "One Lord, one faith, one baptism; one God" (Eph. 4:5–6). The Bible is kept from error by the Spirit of God. It is as fresh and relevant today as it was on any given day in the past. It will be fresh tomorrow. "…the Word [is] God" (John 1:1).

The Bible itself claims to be free from error. It still has the power to convict men of their sins and the power to deliver from sin. The Word is Jesus, who "became flesh and dwelt among us" (John 1:14).

It was the Spirit of God that actually wrote the Bible through men who were surrendered to His will. God Himself is the author, "for prophecy never came by the will of man, but holy men of God spoke as they were moved by the Holy Spirit" (2 Pet. 1:21).

Though first-century persecution, heresy and doubt assailed it, fifty-five hundred handwritten documents have survived. The Bible has endured over two thousand years of constant controversy. Every possible philosophy has assailed it. Most of those have come and gone. As it is written, "The grass withers, the flower fades, but the word of our God stands forever" (Isa. 40:8).

Rather than having lost any of its importance with time, the Bible has actually been found to be more accurate than even thought. Jesus can be found in every book of the Bible from Genesis to Revelation. He has over three hundred names given to Him. An angel announced His name of Jesus (Matt. 1:21; Luke 1:31). It means Savior. Christ means the "Anointed One." Jesus called Himself the "I AM." When Moses approached the burning bush, God spoke to him and said He was the I AM. The religious Jews knew what Jesus meant. They knew quite well that the "I AM" referred to God Himself. It is the reason they crucified Him.

The coming of Jesus had been the hope of every believer. Every generation had wondered and awaited the promised Messiah. Over three hundred times in twenty books of the Bible His coming is prophesied. The fulfilled prophecy helps verify that He is the awaited Messiah. He fulfilled the Scriptures in every detail.

The entire Bible is replete with prophecy. The entire Old Testament is a promise and a celestial guarantee of a coming Savior. The Old Testament conveys the history of the people that carried the seed of this Messiah through the ages. In generation after generation Satan fought to end the lineage of this seed, for he knew what would happen should this seed manifest. He remembered well the prophecy of God in the Garden of Eden.

In Genesis 3:15 God said that Satan's head would be crushed with a certain seed from a woman. He also said that Satan would bruise His heel in the process. This seed was to be Jesus. The bruising was His crucifixion. It was this promise and this seed that stayed alive through the subsequent centuries right in the middle of Satan's wicked maneuvers until that glorious day in Bethlehem.

Fulfilled prophecies help verify the fact that Jesus is the Christ. The particular prophecies are not generalities, but they are complete down to the minutest details. One such prophecy dealt with the very town where Jesus was to be born, Bethlehem. It would receive God Himself. The Bible foretold, "But you, Bethlehem…though you are little among the thousands of Judah, yet out of you shall come forth to Me the One to be Ruler in Israel, whose goings forth are from of old, from everlasting" (Mic. 5:2).

At the time of Jesus' birth Satan worked his evil through King Herod. Herod knew well of the prophecy. He called together the wise men of the day, and when they could not find the baby, he ordered the death of all the infants in the area less than two years of age. He hoped the dead would include Jesus. But an angel had warned Mary and Joseph, and they had fled to safety in Egypt (Matt. 2:13–15). This fulfilled another prophecy: "A voice was heard in Ramah, lamentation, weeping and great mourning, Rachel weeping for her children, refusing to be comforted, because they were no more" (Matt. 2:18).

But regardless of Satan's wickedness, it is written, "For there is born to you this day in the city of David a Savior, who is Christ the Lord" (Luke 2:11).

The following are some of the prophecies found in the Old Testament and verified in the New Testament:

Old Testament	Prophecy	New Testament
Genesis 3:15	Seed of a woman	Matthew 1:20
Isaiah 7:14	Virgin born	Matthew 1:18
Genesis 49:10	Tribe of Judah	Luke 3:23, 33
Micah 5:2	Born in Bethlehem	Matthew 2:1
Psalm 72:10	Given gifts	Matthew 2:11
Jeremiah 31:15	Herod kills babies	Matthew 2:16
Isaiah 7:14	Called Immanuel	Matthew 1:23
Isaiah 40:3	Preceded by messenger	Matthew 3:1–2
Isaiah 35:5–6	Ministry of miracles	Matthew 9:35
Zechariah 9:9	In Jerusalem on a donkey	Luke 19:35–36
Zechariah 9:9	Triumphant entry	John 12:12–14
Psalm 16:10	Resurrection	Acts 2:31
Psalm 68:18	Ascension	Acts 1:9
Psalm 41:9	Betrayed by friend	John 13:21
Zechariah 11:13	Money thrown down	Matthew 27:5
Zechariah 13:7	Forsaken by disciples	Matthew 26:56
Psalm 35:11	Accused by false witness	Matthew 26:60
Isaiah 53:7	Dumb before accuser	Matthew 27:14
Isaiah 53:3	His rejection	John 1:11
Psalm 22:16	Hands, feet pierced	John 20:25
Isaiah 53:5	Wounded, bruised	Matthew 27:26
Isaiah 50:6	Smitten, spit upon	Matthew 27:30
Isaiah 53:12	Crucified with thieves	Matthew 27:38
Psalm 22:18	Garments parted, lots cast	John 19:23–24
Isaiah 44:6	King of Israel	John 1:49
Psalm 22:1	His forsaken cry	Matthew 27:46
Numbers 9:12	No broken bones	John 19:33–36
Zechariah 12:10	Side pierced	John 19:34
Amos 8:9	Darkness over land	Matthew 27:45

According to the Bible there is but one God.

- Deuteronomy 6:4
- Isaiah 44:6–8; 45:5–6; 46:9
- Mark 12:29

- Ephesians 4:5–6
- Malachi 2:10
- 1 Timothy 2:5
- James 2:19
- 1 Corinthians 8:4–6

But we find in the Bible that Jesus is God! Out of His infinite compassion He became a man in the flesh and died for our sins.

- Isaiah 7:14; 9:6; 43:10–11; 45:22
- 1 Timothy 3:16
- 2 Corinthians 5:19
- Colossians 1:15; 2:9
- Revelation 1:8
- Matthew 28:17–20
- Acts 4:10–12
- John 1:1–3, 14; 5:18; 10:30; 14:6, 9–11

Jesus is the Creator:

- John 1:10
- 1 Corinthians 8:6
- Ephesians 3:9
- Hebrews 1:2
- Colossians 1:16–17
- Revelation 10:6; 14:6–7

Jesus became a man:

- Matthew 1:23
- 1 Timothy 3:16
- John 1:10–11, 14; 14:5–10
- Colossians 1:15; 2:8–9

In the Bible God is given many names and designations. Some of His unlimited attributes and qualities are presented in the written Word. Upon close scrutiny, we find that Jesus and God are given the very same designations.

God, the Rock
Deuteronomy 32:1–4
2 Samuel 22:3, 32
Psalm 18:2; 31:3; 78:35; 89:26
Isaiah 44:8

Jesus, the Rock
Isaiah 28:16
Acts 4:11–12
Ephesians 2:20–22
1 Peter 2:6–8

**God, the First and
the Last**
Isaiah 41:4; 43:10; 44:6

**Jesus, the First and
the Last**
Revelation 1:17; 22:13

God Is Coming Again
Zechariah 14:4–5
1 Thessalonians 4:13–18
Revelation 19:11, 16

Jesus Is Coming Again
1 Thessalonians 3:11–13
Matthew 25:31–46
Titus 2:11–13

God, the Shepherd
Psalm 23
Isaiah 40:11
Psalm 100:3

Jesus, the Shepherd
John 10:8–12
1 Peter 2:25; 5:4
Hebrews 13:20

God, the I AM
Exodus 3:13–14

Jesus, the I AM
John 8:5–8

**God, Redeemer
and Savior**
Psalm 78:34–35; 106:21
Isaiah 43:3–11; 44:6; 45:21; 47:4
Luke 1:46–47
Titus 1:1–4; 2:10–13
Jude 25

**Jesus, Redeemer
and Savior**
1 John 4:14
1 Peter 1:10–11; 2:21–24
Acts 20:28
Galatians 3:13
Luke 2:10–11; 24:21–29
John 4:40–42
Philippians 3:20
1 Timothy 1:1–3

God the King	Jesus the King
Psalm 44:4; 47; 74:12	Matthew 2:1–6
Isaiah 43:15; 44:6	Luke 19:32–38; 23:3
Jeremiah 10:10	John 18:37; 19:19–21
Zechariah 14:9	1 Timothy 6:13–16
	Revelation 15:1–4; 19:11–16

The Bible tells us that God alone walks upon the sea (Job 9:8). We find God doing just that in the person of Jesus Christ (Matt. 14:25). The Old Testament tells us that only God can forgive sins (Isa. 43:28). In the New Testament Jesus forgave sins (Mark 2:7). Jesus is the true God (1 John 5:12). Jesus' followers called Him God (John 20:28; Acts 7:59).

God is omnipresent. He can be on earth and in heaven simultaneously (John 3:13). God came in the flesh, yet we find in the Book of Revelation that Jesus sits on the throne (1 Tim. 3:16; Rev. 4:2). Who can understand God, for He says that as high as the heavens are above the earth, so are His ways above our ways, and His thoughts above our thoughts. (See Isaiah 55:8–9.)

The Muslim cannot see the deity of Jesus because he does not believe. He has been led to believe a lie. For the sake of all, especially Muslims, this lie must be exposed.

The Bible recognizes the segment of mankind that Satan has blinded, "whose minds the god of this age has blinded, who do not believe" (2 Cor. 4:3–4). They do not see that Jesus came to give them life in more abundance (John 10:10).

Jesus is not a mere man, but God in the flesh. He can forgive sins and transform lives. He can still calm the troubled sea. He has defeated Satan once and for all on the cross.

The Lord says, "My glory I will not give to another" (Isa. 42:8). There is only one Lord, one God (Deut. 6:4). Christ is that Lord! (Luke 2:11).

The religious scholars of the day asked Jesus who He was. Jesus answered, "Most assuredly, I say to you, before

Abraham was, I AM" (John 8:58). And again, the Bible tells us, "For in Him dwells all the fullness of the Godhead bodily; and you are complete in Him, who is the head of all principality and power" (Col. 2:9–10).

After the apostle John had his heavenly vision, he wrote of what he saw and heard. The angels sang to Jesus, "You are worthy, O Lord, to receive glory and honor and power; for You created all things, and by Your will they exist and were created" (Rev. 4:11).

Isaiah calls Jesus the everlasting Father (Isa. 9:6). The New Testament presents the facts concerning Jesus' life. We have discovered that the Old Testament also contains manifold references to Jesus. Allah may be the Arab name for God, but Muhammad's Qur'an is not of the one true God, for it does not in any way fulfill Scripture. It establishes, develops and takes an altogether different path. It perpetrates clever and destructive lies, tools used by Satan to lure mankind to hell.

Jesus said, "He who has seen Me has seen the Father" (John 14:9). The Bible teaches us, "And He [Jesus] is before all things, and in Him all things consist" (Col. 1:17). The God of the Old Testament, the God of Abraham, Isaac and Jacob, is the same God of the New Testament. God does not change. "Jesus Christ is the same yesterday, today, and forever" (Heb. 13:8).

The physical events of the Old Testament overshadowed the events of the New Testament. God spoke through the prophets the same as He spoke in person.

> For this reason we also thank God without ceasing, because when you received the word of God which you heard from us, you welcomed it not as the word of men, but as it is in truth, the word of God, which also effectively works in you who believe.
>
> —1 Thessalonians 2:13

God is consistent. He does not deceive. When He fore-shadows an event, He does so in truth. Isaac was the son of promise, as was Jesus. Jonah spent three days in the whale; Jesus spent three days in the tomb. Moses was to save his people, as was Jesus. On and on, the entire Old Testament can correlate and foreshadow God's life on earth. It fits no one else. Every Old Testament event is connected to Jesus—every one!

Satan tries to close the door to Jesus for mankind, but Jesus opened a door that no one can shut. Satan wants to destroy us, but Islam and all the death and terror it can contrive will not and cannot remove the saving grace of Jesus Christ. Just as Jacob uncapped the well for the sheep and never put the cover back on, so Jesus has provided us with the well of living water for all to drink. No one can cap this well. Jesus will not fail anyone!

Jesus promises, "I will never leave you nor forsake you" (Heb. 13:5). Islam claims to continue the lineage of the Bible. It claims the Old Testament as its roots. But the Old Testament speaks of a Savior. It speaks of Jesus in various ways. Jesus said, "'I am the Alpha and the Omega, the Beginning and the End,' says the Lord, 'who is and who was and who is to come, the Almighty'" (Rev. 1:8).

15

Why Israel?

The LORD your God has chosen you to be a people for
Himself, a special treasure above all peoples on the
face of the earth.

—DEUTERONOMY 7:6

Diminutive Israel, lodged amid hostile Islamic
neighbors and the sea, is again immersed in adver-
sity and is the focal point of severe tension in the
Mideast. But this tiny country has survived all challenges. It
has been a victim of mass genocide, wars, slavery, occupa-
tions and dispersion. How does a country with such mea-
ger proportions not only survive, but also exert such a
tremendous influence throughout history? Pesky Israel
transcends time and every attempt to put her down.

To understand this phenomenon and to answer the
arresting questions that Israel's unique history suggests, we
must go back to Genesis 3:15. This saga began in the
Garden of Eden after Satan had transgressed God's creation and God had promised Satan that He would send a
Savior to crush his head. "And I will put enmity between

you and the woman, and between your seed and her Seed; He shall bruise your head, and you shall bruise His heel" (Gen. 3:15).

Adam and Eve had sinned because they listened to Satan. As the sin of the individual was held to bring sin and a curse upon the group (as in Joshua 7), so might the righteousness of the individual be expected to procure justification for the group. Thus the need for a Savior (Gen. 18:22–23).[1]

Israel is a country of converging destinies. It is a thorn in the side of Islam, for Israel sits on the holy land, land coveted by Jews, Christians and Muslims. "Israel will exist and will continue to exist until Islam will obliterate it, just as it obliterated others before it. Kill so many Jews that they will eventually abandon Palestine," Imam Hasan al-Bana Ibrahim Sarbal, leader of Islamic Jihad Movement in Palestine, said in a sermon. "Six million descendants of monkeys, these Jews who now rule in all the nations of the world, but their day, too, will come. Allah! Kill them all, do not leave even one!"

Taking this position one step further, Hamas spiritual leader Sheik Ahmad Yasin formulated the concept that Palestine should become the central battlefield for the creation of a nationalist Islamic state—in other words, holy war now. For Hamas, the question of Israel's eventual eradication is central and absolute.

Some Muslims contend that Jesus' ministry was only for the children of Israel and not for all mankind, as Christians believe. On the basis of this argument, they attempt to persuade Christians to become followers of Muhammad, since they claim he alone was a universal prophet for all people for all time.

Isn't it ironic that Israel's capital, Jerusalem, means city of peace? Since Israel was reconstituted as a nation, she has been plagued by bitter disputes. This is a matter of urgency seeing that this conflict could have a polarizing effect on

Christians and Muslims around the world. Therefore God-fearers ought to pray for the peace of Jerusalem as Scripture says in Psalm 122:6.

Peace prospects for Israel seem bleak considering count-less failed peace efforts and continued bitter fighting. Palestinians remember they weren't consulted when the UN partitioned Palestine in 1947. They struggle to come to terms with what seems to them an illegitimate act by the UN when it recognized the state of Israel. The deepening dispute, fueled by spiraling rage and vengeance, causes many to lose hope that there will ever be a just settlement with lasting peace. As hopeless as it seems from a human viewpoint, there are reasons to be encouraged and to believe Almighty God can do the impossible.

After the rebirth of the nation Israel and its recognition by the United Nations in 1948, Arabs launched a war of elimination against the Jews. Nineteen years later the Arab League planned another full-scale attack against Israel, but again Israel survived virtually unscathed. Indeed, she acquired considerable new territory. The UN called on Israel to return all this new land, but Israel has only given back a portion of it.

Numerous attempts have been made since 1967 to nego-tiate a peace settlement, one of the more notable ones being the Oslo Peace Accord. This agreement was meant to mark a milestone in Arab attitudes to Jews, whereby they would recognize Israel's right to be a nation. Arafat agreed to have the Covenant of the PLO and the Charter of the Palestinian National Authority amended to enshrine Israel's right of existence. However, Arab hatred against the Jews proved too intense, and the promised amendments never materialized. Muslim radicals have become frustrated at Arafat's failure to deliver their promised land.

Peace negotiations have reached the critical stage. The Al Aqsa mosque and Dome of the Rock are on or near the place where the Jewish temple once stood. It has been called the most volatile acreage on earth. When the Israelis captured the Al Aqsa mosque in 1967, they knew it held a unique religious status in Islam and that it would invite war. Subsequent riots and terrorism have left thousands dead.

Islamic fundamentalists are determined to gain control over Jerusalem and total control over the Al Aqsa mosque. However, Israel will not relinquish sovereignty of the Temple Mount, her leaders contending that Jerusalem is the capital of Israel, with the Temple Mount at its center, for all eternity.

Since Israel maintains possession of the Temple Mount, the holiest site of the Jews, one would think they would have the privilege of praying there on Jewish holy days. However, Jerusalem's leading Islamic sheikh has objected fiercely to any such suggestion, saying, "We will not stand idly by…not over our dead bodies." The enmity aroused by having holy places on the same piece of ground is understandable, and to some extent unavoidable. It is the animosity between two half-brothers, Isaac and Ishmael, who both claim strong ties with Abraham as a patriarch and spiritual leader.

Another undercurrent that explains why the peace process has failed is the Islamic belief that has circulated widely among Palestinians stating that Muslims will destroy the Jews in the last days. Authoritative Hadith writings quote Muhammad as saying, "The Last Hour would not come unless the Muslims will fight against the Jews and the Muslims would kill them until the Jews would hide themselves behind a stone or a tree, and a stone or a tree would say: Muslim, or the servant of Allah, there is a Jew behind me; come and kill him."[2]

Prospects for peace are dim. Something extraordinary must happen if this deadlock is to be broken. For this we must turn to God. Whether Jew, Christian or Muslim, the common belief is that God will send the Messiah as peace-maker in the last days. According to Muslim belief Al Masih will usher in an era of peace. But the Bible describes the Messiah as the "Prince of Peace." "He shall speak peace to the nations…They shall beat their swords into plowshares" (Zech. 9:10; Isa. 2:4). Could there be some common ground here? Certainly exploring the idea of Messiah and His role in the peace process is worth pursuing.[3]

Satan has kept a perpetual vigil on God's people. He probed for the day and the person that would come to fulfill this prophecy, while God searched for a person worthy to carry this seed. Seven generations elapsed after the Flood, and God finally found a man who was willing to listen to Him and to obey Him. Abraham, who was at first named Abram, became God's vessel, and the saga began.

> Now the LORD had said to Abram: "Get out of your country, from your family and from your father's house, to a land that I will show you. I will make you a great nation; I will bless you and make your name great; and you shall be a blessing. I will bless those who bless you, and I will curse him who curses you; and in you all the families of the earth shall be blessed."
> —GENESIS 12:1–3

Then the Lord God made a covenant with Abraham and his people. The Lord said unto Abraham, "Lift your eyes now and look from the place where you are—northward, southward, eastward, and westward; for all the land which you see I give to you and your descendants forever. And I will make your descendants as the dust of the earth; so that if a man could number the dust of the earth, then your descendants also could be numbered. Arise, walk in the land through its length and its width, for I give it to you" (Gen. 13:14–17).

The Lord had spoken this promise to Abraham when he was already seventy-five years old (Gen. 12:4). So he set out with his wife Sarai (Sarah), and they went to the Promised Land of Canaan, present-day Israel. In this land their lives revolved around the promise of a son that would carry the seed. The seed passed from Abraham, through King David and on for generations to the prophecy's fulfillment in the birth of Jesus.

The Old Testament comprises this tumultuous history of the land, the lineage and Israel's on-going relationship with God. This promise of a Savior burned in the hearts of the Jewish people century after century. They longed for the day when Israel's adversaries would be forever silenced.

God called Israel His elect: "For Jacob My servant's sake, and Israel My elect, I have even called you by your name", (Isa. 45:4).

This land and this promise are at the root of the Middle East difficulty today. Both the Jews and the Muslims claim this birthright and the land that goes with it. This is where Satan manufactures his Qur'anic distortion and the entire divergence begins. Satan begins with truth, with Scripture, and then creates his Islamic lie. But no matter the foe, no one can or will ever change God's Word or defeat Israel. She is God's chosen nation; for better or for worse, whether they themselves obey God or not, they are married to His infinite plan.

The conflict and unique situation we see in Palestine began because Abraham fathered two sons. One was the son of a bondwoman, and the other was God's son of promise. The bondwoman's son was called Ishmael, from whom descended the Arabs. The son of promise, Isaac, fathered the Jews. God favored the seed of Isaac over the seed of Ishmael. Isaac's son Jacob was later renamed Israel.

Say to them, "Thus says the Lord GOD: 'On the day

when I chose Israel and raised My hand in an oath to the descendants of the house of Jacob, and made Myself known to them in the land of Egypt, I raised My hand in an oath to them saying, I am the LORD your God.'"

—EZEKIEL 20:5

Ishmael was born because Abraham and Sarah did not wait upon the Lord for the son of promise. "Now we, brethren, as Isaac was, are children of promise...But he who was of the bondwoman was born according to the flesh" (Gal. 4:28, 23).

Abraham was getting up in years, and he must have wondered just how this son of promise would be born. Years passed, and he and his wife only grew older. Still more time elapsed, and yet no son. Ten years after the promise Sarah was still barren. Impatiently, Sarah gave her handmaiden Hagar to Abraham that she might bear him children. Sarah's natural impatience and reasoning overcame God's promise in her mind and heart. Abraham went in to Hagar, and she conceived Ishmael. Abraham must have wondered if this son would be the promised one. But the Lord came to Abraham in a vision and told him, "'Do not be afraid, Abram. I am your shield, your exceedingly great reward.' But Abram said, 'Lord GOD, what will You give me, seeing I go childless'...Then Abram said, 'Look, You have given me no offspring'...And behold, the word of the LORD came to him, saying, 'This one [Ishmael] shall not be your heir'" (Gen. 15:1–4).

When Abraham was ninety-nine years old, the Lord again spoke to him, and this time God changed his name:

No longer shall your name be called Abram, but your name shall be Abraham; for I have made you the father of many nations. I will make you exceedingly fruitful; and I will make nations of you, and kings shall

146

come from you...Also I give to you and your descendants after you the land in which you are a stranger,
all the land of Canaan, as an everlasting possession;
and I will be their God.

—GENESIS 17:5–6, 8

And then God told Abraham, "You shall keep My
covenant, you and your descendants after you throughout
their generations" (Gen. 17:9).

God also changed Sarai's name to Sarah. He told her
that she would be the mother of nations and kings.
Quite expectedly, due to his age, Abraham laughed at
God. He decidedly felt that there could be no child.
After all, they were now very old and well beyond their
child-bearing years.

But the power of God became manifest and the
prophecy of Israel made true: "No, Sarah your wife shall
bear you a son, and you shall call his name Isaac; I will
establish My covenant with him for an everlasting
covenant" (Gen. 17:19).

Also, at this very same time, God blessed Ishmael. He
promised to make a nation of him also. "And as for Ishmael,
I have heard you. Behold, I have blessed him, and will make
him fruitful, and will multiply him exceedingly" (Gen.
17:20).

Then God turned to Abraham again and said, "But My
covenant I will establish with Isaac, whom Sarah shall bear
to you at this set time next year" (Gen. 17:21).

Then three angels appeared to Abraham and told him to
find his wife Sarah and again they told him that she would
have a son (Gen. 18:2–10). God's work is readily apparent
here, for Abraham and Sarah were well stricken with age.
God heard their laughter and knew their unbelief. He said
to them, "Is anything too hard for the Lord?...Sarah shall
have a son" (Gen. 18:14).

Sarah continued to laugh. But after she had heard the word of the Lord she became fearful.

Years of waiting on the Lord had not been in vain, for God finally visited Sarah and she bore a son at her appointed time. Sarah said, "God has made me laugh, and all who hear will laugh with me" (Gen. 21:6).

Abraham was now one hundred years old. The son was named Isaac as God had commanded (Gen. 21:1–3, 5).

Soon after Isaac was born, Ishmael's true nature became apparent. As Ishmael grew to adolescence, he began to mock Isaac. "But, as he who was born according to the flesh then persecuted him who was born according to the Spirit, even so it is now" (Gal. 4:29).

Isaac endured the persecution of Ishmael and was faithful until death. But then Ishmael also began to mock Sarah. Sarah became angry and asked Abraham to cast the bond-woman and the insolent Ishmael out. Abraham became grief stricken, for Ishmael, though troublesome, was still his son.

But then God commanded him, "Do not let it be displeasing in your sight because of the lad or because of the bondwoman. Whatever Sarah has said to you, listen to her voice; for in Isaac your seed shall be called. Yet I will also make a nation of the son of the bondwoman, because he is your seed" (Gen. 21:12–13).

Thus Ishmael began the Arab race. God was not content to use Ishmael to bring about the promised blessing, for Ishmael was born by will of the flesh and unbelief. His descendants became Gentiles, to whom the promise is now also open if they but believe on the fulfillment of God's promise to Abraham.

And it came to pass that God again called upon Abraham and tested his obedience to the utmost. He asked Abraham to take this only son of promise, Isaac, the son he had awaited for so many years, and sacrifice him. He was to kill his son in the prescribed manner of a burnt offering.

Abraham unflinchingly obeyed God and prepared an altar on which to sacrifice Isaac. God sent an angel to intervene just as Abraham raised the knife to kill him. God then provided Abraham and Isaac a ram, which they killed and sacrificed instead.

This was a foreshadowing of God giving His own Son.

> For God so loved the world that He gave his only begotten Son, that whoever believes in Him should not perish but have everlasting life.
>
> —JOHN 3:16

The Bible tells us, "By faith Abraham, when he was tested, offered up Isaac, and he who received the promises offered up his only begotten son" (Heb. 11:17).

Abraham was willing to sacrifice his own son. For this reason he found great favor in God's eyes, and Abraham was further blessed. The qualities that God found admirable in Abraham were righteousness, humbleness and that he was near to God.

"In your seed all the nations of the earth shall be blessed, because you have obeyed My voice" (Gen. 22:18). Abraham grew older, and as he neared death he gave all that he had to Isaac.

Jesus, the promised Savior, was born into the tribe of Judah, one of the twelve tribes of Abraham (Gen. 3:15; Gal. 3:16).

The Lord said, "The scepter shall not depart from Judah" (Gen. 49:10).

"I will bring forth descendants from Jacob, and from Judah an heir of My mountains" (Isa. 65:9).

These promises have come from God Himself. No one can change them. It is written: "Moreover I will appoint a place for My people Israel, and will plant them, that they may dwell in a place of their own and move no more... And who is like Your people, like Israel, the one nation on the earth whom God went to redeem for Himself as a people, to make for Himself a name...For You have made Your people Israel Your very own people forever" (2 Sam. 7:10, 23–24).

The Bible tells us that by virtue of His promise God fights for Israel (Deut. 3:22). "The LORD will cause your enemies who rise against you to be defeated before your face; they shall come out against you one way and flee before you seven ways" (Deut. 28:7).

Satan's final undoing was the birth of Jesus, the very promise of Genesis 3:15 fulfilled. The seed that was carried and protected came to be despite all the efforts of Satan. The King of heaven was born on earth. He was born into the family of Jesse as prophesied: "There shall come forth a Rod from the stem of Jesse" (Isa. 11:1)

This very promise given to Abraham is now passed on to all who believe on Jesus. "And if you are Christ's, then you are Abraham's seed, and heirs according to the promise" (Gal. 3:29).

To those of us that are far removed from the actual bloodshed, the Middle East can seem like a cauldron of confusion. But anyone familiar with Scripture can see that all the pieces fit together quite well. They fulfill all the predictions made thousands of years ago. All history revolves around the Jews, because one man obeyed God. The world and Israel are inextricably intertwined. The Bible reviews their origins, outlines their history and unfolds their future.

If it had not been for the Lord's unconditional promise of preserving Israel that He gave to Abraham (Gen. 12:1–3), confirmed to Isaac (Gen. 26:3–4), and then ratified to Jacob (Gen. 28:13–15), Israel may have disappeared from the face of the earth long ago.[4] The Jews are God's covenant people. Whatever the Jews do, good or bad, God's promise must stand.

Where there is a possession there must be a possessor. In this case, the possessor had already been identified by God Himself as the descendants of Isaac, Abraham's promised son. (Compare Genesis 22:15–19.) Neither Ramses, Haman nor Hitler could eradicate the Jews. God made a promise, and that is why God has been obliged to preserve the Jews for the past four thousand years.[5]

Islam claims that the Jews are unrighteous invaders. Such falsehood should never become the basis for any cross-cultural treaty. The truth can be easily established scripturally and also on a historical basis. The Arabs only assume their posture because they have been deceived by a satanic warp. Palestine was not first settled by the Jews after World War II, but it has been their home for thirty-five hundred years. The Jewish homeland has existed in an unbroken lineage from Abraham. And it is not the Arab people that are the real enemy here, but Satan and the lies he has sold them.

The Jews have not always been obedient. Consequently they were dispersed and scattered to the four winds, all according to prophecy. And it was prophesied that at the appointed time, God would gather the Jews and reestablish Zion. Curiously enough, in the mid-1940s, while Hitler burned and gassed six million Jews, they inexplicably began this return to Palestine from the four corners of the earth.

Efforts were made to stop them. The British leaders told them they could have Uganda, trying in vain to keep them out of the oil-rich Middle East. But still, and against all probability and against all opposition, they continued to come by all means available. They fought against impossible odds. They won incomprehensible victories, while unrestrained efforts were made by overwhelming forces to keep them out. When they finally arrived, they survived an all-out effort to drive them out. But despite all efforts, in 1948 they again became a nation.

This was not even necessarily the will of the Jews, but that of Almighty God. He had predicted, "Behold, I will gather them out of all countries where I have driven them in My anger, in My fury, and in great wrath; I will bring them back to this place, and I will cause them to dwell safely" (Jer. 32:37).

God had once prophesied that whoever would strike the Shepherd would be scattered. Jesus is the Good Shepherd, and when the Jews killed Him due to their unbelief, the Lord had scattered them. So prophecy was once again fulfilled: "Strike the Shepherd, and the sheep will be scattered" (Zech. 13:7).

On May 14, 1948, David Ben-Gurion announced Israel's rebirth as a nation. The celebration was short-lived, for immediately the surrounding Islamic states attacked with a fury. Their objective was to drown the Jews in the Mediterranean "like dogs." But by the time a cease-fire was announced, Israel had already gained back half of its land.

After the Jewish resettlement, anyone that came against them was dealt a quick and decisive setback. The Bible tells us that from this point on that anyone that attacks Israel will be dealt blows with incredible swiftness and that the battles shall not last long.

As Israel resettled the land and grew in prominence, the Muslims again conspired to drive them out of Palestine. They gathered an overwhelming force against them, and then in 1967 attacked them in what is now called the "Six Day War." In merely six days the attackers were dealt a blow so severe that it crippled them for years. That instantaneous sting again only confirmed God's Word. It gave credence to the fact that Israel was back to stay. As a result of this war, Israel again regained more of its land.

We can see additional evidences of God's Word and the swift retribution that was prophesied against Israel's enemies. When Syria attacked Israel with their Soviet-backed air force but a decade ago, the Israelis shot down eighty enemy planes without losing a single plane!

The Jews had never forgotten their homeland though dispersed, exiled or persecuted. For thirty-five centuries this theme of Palestine has been centrally knit in Jewish literature. Jews worldwide revere the Old Testament, Jerusalem and its ancient temple. Islam and its disruptions began only fourteen hundred years ago. Along with the Bible, history itself shines an unmistakable light on Satan's big lie.

The Jews had been beaten down many times by forces of the Assyrians, Babylonians, Egyptians, Persians, Greeks, Byzantines, Arabs, Romans, Kurds, Mumluks and the Mongols. They've been killed and scattered, but Satan has never been able to destroy or remove God's chosen from the land He has given them. Despite all odds and tumultuous destructions, the Jews remain to testify to God's unerring Word. Under the earthly rule of foreign kings and peoples too numerous to mention, the Jews cling stubbornly to the Holy Land. The Jewish mind, culture and belief systems are synonymous with this position. They have lived and died for these Old Testament beliefs. This noble heritage is documented and irreversible.

Another very interesting point that needs further consideration is biblical nationalism. It is the success or failure of a country by virtue of its relationship to Israel.

‑God says, "Israel was holiness to the LORD, the firstfruits of His increase. All that devour him will offend; disaster will come upon them" (Jer. 2:3).

Therefore a country's stance with Israel is of paramount importance, not because of any worldly consideration, but because of God's Word. History itself revolves around Israel.

It is God's will for any country that does not align itself with Israel to be eventually destroyed. It has happened before. Various nations that have come against Israel are no longer on the planet, nor are their peoples. When the

Egyptians' god-king Ramses assumed the posture of being god over Israel, God destroyed all that he had. Many such instances can be found.

No one will stand against Israel and survive.

> It shall happen in that day that I will seek to destroy all the nations that come against Jerusalem. And it shall happen in that day that I will make Jerusalem a very heavy stone for all peoples: all who would heave it away will surely be cut in pieces, though all nations of the earth are gathered against it.
>
> —ZECHARIAH 12:3

> For the nation and the kingdom which shall not serve you shall perish, and those nations shall be utterly ruined.
>
> —ISAIAH 60:12

Islam also lays claim to God's promise. This is not unusual. Satan from the very beginning lusted after what was the Lord's. In heaven he wanted to be worshiped as God. He still works to steal and destroy that which is of the Lord, but the Lord Jesus Christ has compromised him. All prophecy has been fulfilled, and Jesus was born in Israel.

Other countries are only mentioned in Scripture in so much as they come into contact with Israel. The nature of the Messiah and the role of Israel are inseparable.[6] In the prediction, birth and various experiences of the Messiah, Israel's history is enacted, but with one difference. Where Israel failed, the Messiah succeeds; what Israel was meant to be, the Messiah is: the perfect servant of God.[7]

16

People of the Book

> Those who reject (Truth), among the People of the
> Book and among the Polytheists, will be in Hell-Fire,
> to dwell therein (for aye). They are the worst of crea-
> tures.
>
> —SÜRAH 98:6

Jews and Christians are called the "People of the
Book" in the Qur'an. Muhammad taught that under
no circumstances are they to be trusted. They are
respected for getting Allah's limited revelations, but are
condemned because after receiving them, Muhammad
said they distorted and rejected his final revelation.

Christians are viewed as more docile and easy-going
than Jews. Muhammad taught contempt for Christians, but
all the more for the Jews who resisted him, mocked him
and called him an unprincipled impostor. He could not
convert them. They painted him in the blackest of colors.
He called them dogs. When he won a military skirmish, he
would terrorize and behead the Jewish men. He sold the
women into slavery, and some he kept for his own pleasure

as concubines. There is a saying in Islam: "If a Muslim is with two Jews, the Jews will try to kill him."

Muhammad said that the Christian is actually attracted to Islam because it sets the record straight concerning Jesus. The Christians are called the descendants of the hateful ones, who are the Jews. Muslims are called upon to hate and terrorize Jews. The daily news reports testify to this edict.

The Qur'an states, "For the iniquity of the Jews We made unlawful for them certain (foods) good and wholesome which had been lawful for them; in that they hindered many from Allah's way—that they took usury, and that they devoured men's substance wrongfully" (Sürah 4:160–161).

Islam holds that there were twenty-eight prophets that originally served Allah, but that they were not Jewish. They teach that the prophets, Adam to Jesus, were actually Muslims. They claimed that the Jews derailed the truth when they failed to accept Muhammad as the final prophet.

Adam is recognized as the first man and also the first prophet to whom Allah revealed himself. It also contends that the apostles of Jesus were Muslims. Islam claims that Moses was sent to save the children of Ishmael's nephew from the evil pharaoh in Egypt. There are said to have been five Major Prophets that preceded Muhammad. They are Adam, Moses, Noah, Abraham and Jesus—all Muslims.

17

Israel and Jesus Today

Brethren, my heart's desire and prayer to God for
Israel is that they may be saved.

—Romans 10:1

The West for the most part is Judeo-Christian. What
does the Bible say concerning the differences
between the Jews and the Christians? If the promise
was given to the Jews, how did the Gentiles receive it?
America was founded on biblical principles. It has stood for
Israel and has had a great measure of success, but there still
remains a dichotomy between the Jew and the Christian.

Israel had awaited the Messiah. When He finally came in
a humble way, they did not recognize Him. The Jewish
religious leaders met Him with indifference. Israel, God's
firstborn, rejected their birthright by turning down
Abraham's blessing. But God would be served.

On such an account Jesus told this parable:

A certain man gave a great supper and invited many,
and sent his servant at supper time to say to those who

were invited, "Come, all things are now ready." But they all with one accord began to make excuses…So that servant came and reported these things to his master. Then the master of the house, being angry, said to his servant, "Go out quickly into the streets and lanes of the city, and bring in here the poor and the maimed and the lame and the blind." And the servant said, "Master, it is done as you commanded, and still there is room." Then the master said to the servant, "Go out into the highways and hedges, and compel them to come in, that my house may be filled."

—LUKE 14:16–22

God will be worshiped, and His house will be full. Now the Gentiles are receiving the blessing meant for Israel. The Bible teaches that before the end comes, the Jewish people will return to Jesus and a remnant of them will be saved: "Though the number of the children of Israel be as the sand of the sea, the remnant will be saved" (Rom. 9:27).

The Jews also try to attain to God by works, by adherence to the Law. They use their own efforts as the only hope of their tomorrow. Only Jesus was able to live a sinless life and be the pure sacrifice for sin. He alone was able to do the Father's will. He alone is the Savior.

What shall we say then? That Gentiles, who did not pursue righteousness, have attained to righteousness, even the righteousness of faith; but Israel, pursuing the law of righteousness, has not attained to the law of righteousness. Why? Because they did not seek it by faith, but as it were, by the works of the law. For they stumbled at that stumbling stone. As it is written: "Behold, I lay in Zion a stumbling stone and rock of offense, and whoever believes on Him [Jesus] will not be put to shame."

—ROMANS 9:30–33

The Jews had asked Jesus who He was. He responded by saying, "I and My Father are One" (John 10:30).

The response of the Jewish religious leaders was to pick up stones, for they saw this statement as blasphemous. They correctly perceived what He was saying. Yet Jesus was not blaspheming, for what He said was the truth: before them indeed did stand the eternal Messiah.[1]

Because the Jews rejected Jesus, the Gentiles have received the blessing and have been adopted into the royal family, "that the blessing of Abraham might come upon the Gentiles in Christ Jesus" (Gal. 3:14).

> I was found by those that did not seek Me; I was made manifest to those who did not ask for Me…All day long I have stretched out My hands to a disobedient and contrary people.
>
> —Romans 10:19–20

And God continued to speak to Israel: "The Gentiles shall come to your light" (Isa. 60:3).

Despite the rejection of God by Israel, He has demonstrated His love and His fidelity by never divorcing Himself from them. We find that the God's rejection of Israel is partial: "Has God cast away His people? Certainly not!…Even so then, at this present time there is a remnant according to the election of grace…What then? Israel has not obtained what it seeks; but the elect have obtained it, and the rest were blinded. Just as it is written, 'God has given them a spirit of stupor, eyes that they should not see and ears that they should not hear, to this very day'" (Rom. 11:1, 5, 7–8).

The Lord promises that He did not forget Israel: "Remember these, O Jacob, and Israel, for you are My servant; I have formed you, you are My servant; O Israel, you will not be forgotten by Me!" (Isa. 44:21).

Israel is analogous to the olive tree in the Bible. It is written in the Bible that branches of the tree were broken off. This refers to the nonbelievers. Then branches of the Gentiles are grafted in.

"It [the gospel] is the power of God to salvation for everyone who believes, for the Jew first and also for the Greek" (Rom. 1:16). God tells the Gentiles not to boast against Israel as a consequence, but to uphold her. God has told the Christians to leave Israel be since they do not support the root, but that the root supports both the Jews and the Gentiles. The Christians have a compelling reason to show love to and to uphold Israel.

> Because of unbelief they [the branches] were broken off, and you stand by faith. Do not be haughty, but fear. For if God did not spare the natural branches, He may not spare you either. Therefore consider the goodness and severity of God: on those who fell, severity; but toward you, goodness, if you continue in His goodness. Otherwise you also will be cut off. And they also, if they do not continue in unbelief, will be grafted in, for God is able to graft them in again. For if you were cut out of the olive tree which is wild by nature, and were grafted contrary to nature into a cultivated olive tree, how much more will these, who are natural branches, be grafted into their own olive tree?
> —ROMANS 11:20–24

God will not completely remove the promise from Israel. Though Christians should consider Jews as temporarily out of God's will, they will continue to be blessed as a result of the great deeds of their forefathers.

The duration of Israel's rejection is temporary:

> For I do not desire, brethren, that you should be

ignorant of this mystery, lest you should be wise in your own opinion, that blindness in part has happened to Israel until the fullness of the Gentiles has come in. And so all Israel will be saved, as it is written: "The Deliverer will come out of Zion, and He will turn away ungodliness from Jacob; for this is My covenant with them, when I take away their sins." Concerning the gospel they are enemies for your sake, but concerning the election they are beloved for the sake of the fathers. For the gifts and the calling of God are irrevocable. For as you were once disobedient to God, yet have now obtained mercy through their disobedience, even so these also have now been disobedient, that through the mercy shown you they may also obtain mercy.

—Romans 11:25–31

All through the Old Testament God had dealt with Israel. They always prospered when they obeyed God. They prospered in mighty ways. They were given gifts and promises that were select. When they fell away from God and sought to make their own way, they fell from grace. Though it be palatable or not, the Word of God prophesied a Deliverer for Israel. They rejected Him, but the Word of God reigns supreme.

The Bible commands, "But be doers of the word, and not hearers only, deceiving yourselves" (James 1:22).

The following verses are fitting for Christians and Jews alike: "Incline your ear unto my sayings. Do not let them depart from your eyes; keep them in the midst of your heart for they are life to those who find them, and health to all their flesh" (Prov. 4:20–22). "But whoever listens to me will dwell safely, and will be secure, without fear of evil" (Prov. 1:33).

18

Justification and Solution

Go therefore and make disciples of all the nations...
teaching them to observe all things that I have commanded you; and lo, I [Jesus] am with you always, even
to the end of the age.

—MATTHEW 28:19–20

A s a Muslim is commanded to spread terror and
death among nonbelievers, so a Christian is commanded to sow the seeds of truth and to preach
Jesus Christ to a dying world. The dawn of the so-called
Aquarian age opened the door to the humanistic notion
that all religions are basically good and speak of the same
true God. The man-made doctrine claims that as mankind
evolves, the many various religions will also evolve toward
one another in the growing knowledge of science.

The Bible warns of following such wisdom of man. This
mortal savvy may reach lofty proportions, as it did in the
Tower of Babel days, but God will not be mocked. The true

God will have a people, and He will be served. To serve God is the only chance mankind has against the onslaught of deception and evil that grows ever perilously in the Middle East, or anywhere else for that matter. So many "-isms," so many ways deluge humanity today.

Jesus simply announced the truth: "I am the way" (John 14:6).

This truth must be preached in the face of a doubting intelligentsia, as well as in the face of intimidating Islam. God's people should be obedient in the face of all opposition, no matter how the world views them or ridicules them. Noah built his ark in the midst of dry land. He worked on it for one hundred years. During this time all who approached him ridiculed him.

> For it is written: "I will destroy the wisdom of the wise, and bring to nothing the understanding of the prudent." Where is the wise? Where is the scribe? Where is the disputer of this age? Has not God made foolish the wisdom of this world? For since, in the wisdom of God, the world through wisdom did not know God, it pleased God through foolishness of the message preached to save those who believe...Because the foolishness of God is wiser than men, and the weakness of God is stronger than men...But God has chosen the foolish things of the world to put to shame the wise.
> —1 CORINTHIANS 1:19–21, 25, 27

God is not man's order supplier. If He chooses a way that does not conform or agree with the prevalent notions of the day or with the religions of the world, so be it.

The Bible says, "For the message of the cross is foolishness to those who are perishing, but to us who are being saved it is the power of God" (1 Cor. 1:18).

This cross compromised and defeated Satan. It holds up

against Islam. It must be preached. It is the hope of mankind. There are those that will hear—and sadly, as always—there are those that won't. As for Satan, he will continue his destructive ways until the end. The hope of mankind must be lifted up for all to see in the face of death, persecution or terror.

Jesus said, "Now is the judgment of the world; now the ruler of this world will be cast out. And I, if I am lifted up from the earth, will draw all peoples to Myself" (John 12:31–32).

If Jesus is lifted up, all who yearn for the truth can see Him. All who seek love can find Him. All who suffer and are heavy-laden can take shelter in Him. There is no way to water down truth. When there is a terminal malignancy, a surgeon operates as soon as he can. He cuts swiftly and deeply. He tries to save the life of the patient. He removes the tumor. As the tentacles of Islam reach about the earth, threaten life and cause death, the Word of God must cut quickly and precisely. If the Word of the Lord is spoken and carried about, it will slice away the lies and bring light to the world.

> Then Jesus spoke to them again, saying, "I am the light of the world. He who follows Me shall not walk in darkness, but have the light of life."
>
> —JOHN 8:12

With Jesus we can find the way, the truth and the life (John 14:6). It is a more excellent way (1 Cor. 12:31). Islam has darkened much of the world. Islam hates love, Jesus as God and Christianity. It wants to destroy them.

The Bible tells us, "And this is the condemnation, that the light has come into the world, and men loved darkness rather than light, because their deeds were evil" (John 3:19–20).

No mind, no power, no religion, no threat can derail the works of Jesus Christ. He is the Resurrection life, the

Resurrection power. Islam is a very real threat to the eternal life of the Muslim. This threat can be overcome by Jesus. May those who truly seek God find the door to salvation and the everlasting life it contains. The Word must be brought to bear. His ways must be seen. His lamp must be put on the housetop and on the highest hills. The death threats must be drowned out by praise for the Lord!

To the humanitarian that feels he is in charge of his own destiny, it is written, "'For My thoughts are not your thoughts, nor your ways My ways,' says the LORD. 'For as far as the heavens are higher than the earth, so are My ways higher than your ways, and My thoughts than your thoughts'" (Isa. 55:8–9).

May every man, woman, child, every Muslim find Jesus. The peace of Jesus is like the eye of the hurricane, which flourishes in the midst of the tempest.

"For the law of the Spirit of life in Christ Jesus has made me free from the law of sin and death" (Rom. 8:2). "And you shall know the truth, and the truth shall make you free" (John 8:32).

Jesus does not force anyone to love or to follow Him. He does not threaten anyone with death should they refuse. He does not command that those who do not believe be killed, but that they should be loved. He allows all to make the choice. Should anyone find the fire of hell, it is of his or her own choice. He only waits for all His wayward children with open arms of love.

Islam allows for no contradictory view. One must simply surrender to Allah or be killed. A loaded gun is held to the head. If the wrong decision is made, bang! Jesus is the wrong decision in Islam. It brings death.

Jesus said, "He who does not gather with Me scatters" (Luke 11:23).

The bondage of Islam can be overcome very easily with Jesus. This is the same Jesus that overcame death, so the threat of death is no longer a peril. Satan may succeed in killing a body, but once one has surrendered to Jesus, Satan can no longer get that person's soul, which is the real death.

Paul wrote, "So when this corruptible has put on incorruption, and this mortal has put on immortality, then shall be brought to pass the saying that is written: 'Death is swallowed up in victory. O Death, where is your sting? O Hades, where is your victory?'...But thanks be to God, who gives us the victory through our Lord Jesus Christ" (1 Cor. 15:54–57).

Jesus has given us weaponry to stand in the face of the Qur'anic madness.

> Put on the whole armor of God, that you may be able to stand against the wiles of the devil...Therefore take up the whole armor of God, that you may be able to withstand in the evil day, and having done all, to stand. Stand therefore, having girded your waist with truth, having put on the breastplate of righteousness, and having shod your feet with the preparation of the gospel of peace; above all, taking the shield of faith with which you will be able to quench the fiery darts of the wicked one. And take the helmet of salvation, and the sword of the Spirit, which is the word of God; praying always with all prayer and supplication in the Spirit, being watchful to this end with all perseverance and supplication for all the saints—and for me, that utterance may be given to me, that I may open my mouth boldly to make known the mystery of the gospel.
> —EPHESIANS 6:11, 13–20

This book has made tremendous implications for those of the Muslim faith. It is a spiritual wickedness that assails them. Without Jesus the fundamentalists will be helplessly compelled to carry on Satan's murderous affairs of terror and confusion.

But this book also conveys acute questions and a significant challenge for the Christian also. Has God left us alone? Are we cast helplessly adrift in the confusion? Have we nothing to do but await the spread of this insidious evil? Is there a sensible course that can be adopted?

Love is not a sentimental weakness as Muhammad preached. God's love is the only solution. It is powerful. Love heals and binds. Jesus is love incarnate. He is the solution.

> Beloved, let us love one another, for love is of God; and everyone who loves is born of God and knows God. He who does not love does not know God, for God is love. In this the love of God was manifested toward us, that God has sent His only begotten Son into the world, that we might live through Him. In this is love, not that we loved God, but that He loved us and sent His Son to be the propitiation for our sins.
> —1 JOHN 4:7–10

TO THE TERRORIST

Ayatollah Khomeini had declared, "Even if Salman Rushdie (author of *The Satanic Verses*) repents and becomes the most pious man of all time, it is incumbent upon every Muslim to take everything he has, his life and his wealth, and send him to hell." In contrast, the Bible offers forgiveness to all. Christ even died to redeem those who hated Him and asked His Father to forgive those who crucified Him (Luke 23:34).

To those of you who think Christians are your enemy, Christians love you. Jesus loves you. America loves you. But America can't save you, nor can Christians save you. America didn't save Christians. Jesus saved Christians. In America Christians are free to worship and love Jesus. Muslims are free in America. Jesus gives us the strength to love each other and Muslims through His Holy Spirit. The truth in the Word of God reveals that God has chosen to manifest Himself to humans in ways we could understand. We can understand the term *father*, and God is the supreme Father. We understand the concept of a Son, and God came to us as the Son, to gather His sheep that went astray and to give them the gift of salvation. And we all understand Spirit. His Spirit comes to us like the sunshine of the sun, with the light of truth, for Jesus said, "I am the light of the world. He who follows Me shall not walk in darkness, but have the light of life" (John 8:12).

After His resurrection Jesus sent His Holy Spirit to anyone who believed with all his or her heart, and all those that receive His Holy Spirit are baptized into His spiritual body of love. There is but one God, and His name is Jesus, the name above every other name. No one comes to the Father but through the Son. Try Him to see if He isn't true. Try Him with all your heart. Knock, and it shall be opened to you.

> There is no fear in love; but perfect love casts out fear, because fear involves torment. But he who fears has not been made perfect in love. We love Him because He first loved us. If someone says, "I love God," and hates his brother, he is a liar; for he who does not love his brother whom he has seen, how can he love God whom he has not seen? And this commandment we have from Him: that he who loves God must also love his brother.
>
> —1 JOHN 4:18–21

> He who says he is in the light, and hates his brother, is in darkness until now. He who loves his brother abides in the light, and there is no cause for stumbling in him. But he who hates his brother is in darkness and walks in darkness, and does not know where he is going, because the darkness has blinded his eyes.
>
> —1 JOHN 2:9–11

> We know that we have passed from death to life, because we love the brethren. He who does not love his brother abides in death. Whoever hates his brother is a murderer, and you know that no murderer has eternal life abiding in Him. By this we know love, because He laid down His life for us. And we also ought to lay down our lives for the brethren.
>
> —1 JOHN 3:14–16

The terrorist denounces love as weak. He answers with *jihad*. But God has given us another answer. Every terrorist can be saved from this wicked course Satan has set. God has chosen the cross as His plan of salvation. Rather than terrorize and kill unbelievers, Jesus died for them out of His immeasurable love. One needs only to accept this love with a sincere heart and follow God's plan of salvation. The Bible tells just how important love is.

> Though I speak with the tongues of men and of angels, but have not love, I have become as sounding brass or a clanging cymbal. And though I have the gift of prophecy, and understand all mysteries and all knowledge, and though I have all faith, so that I could remove mountains, but have not love, I am nothing. And though I bestow all my goods to feed the poor, and though I give my body to be burned, but have not love, it profits me nothing. Love suffers long and is kind; love does not envy; love does not parade itself, is not puffed up; does not behave rudely, does not seek its own, is not provoked, thinks no evil; does not rejoice in iniquity, but rejoices in truth; bears all things, believes all things, hopes all things, endures all things. Love never fails.
>
> —1 CORINTHIANS 13:1–8

TO THE CHRISTIAN

Who shall bring a charge against God's elect? It is
God who justifies. Who is he who condemns? It is
Christ who died, and furthermore is also risen, who
is even at the right hand of God, who also makes
intercession for us. Who shall separate us from the
love that is in Christ? Shall tribulation, or distress,
or persecution, or famine, or nakedness, or peril, or
sword? As it is written: "For Your sake we are killed
all day long; we are accounted as sheep for the
slaughter." Yet in all these things we are more than
conquerors through Him who loved us. For I am
persuaded that neither death nor life, nor angels,
nor principalities nor powers, nor things present
nor things to come, nor height nor depth, nor any
other created thing, shall be able to separate us from
the love of God which is in Christ Jesus our Lord.
—Romans 8:33–39

Christians need to praise God. God says that He inhabits
the praises of His people (Ps. 22:3). If Christians truly give
God honor and praise, He will stand before us in all things.
The Bible says, "Let everything that has breath praise the
Lord" (Ps. 150:6). Our breath speaks in Jesus' name. The
Lord commands, "And whatever you do in word or deed, do
all in the name of the Lord Jesus" (Col. 3:17).

Christians must unite in prayer and get in touch with
God. "Through God we will do valiantly, for it is He who
shall tread down our enemies" (Ps. 60:12).

The Word of God is absolute. The Jews awaited a Savior
with a sword who would come to conquer their enemies.
Jesus came with that sword. No sword is more powerful
than the Word of God. It has spoken universes into exis-

170

tence. It has spun stars and planets across the galaxies. Nothing can stand before the Word of God. Satan's lies pale before it. In our book, a modest sampling of God's Word has focused in on Islamic *jihad* and easily shown it for what it really is.

The Bible, in its childlike simplicity, contains every answer mankind needs. Many nuggets of gold can be found in it. It not only sheds light on the problems, but also gives the solutions.

God told Joshua, "This Book of the Law shall not depart from your mouth, but you shall meditate in it day and night, that you may observe to do according to all that is written in it. For then you will make your way prosperous, and then you will have good success" (Josh. 1:8).

Mankind cringes from the onslaught of Satan's terror and confusion. The walls of truth need rebuilding. In the days of Nehemiah the walls of Jerusalem were utterly torn down. The enemy rejoiced. The enemy terrorized all who would even consider repairing it. Things seemed hopeless. The enemy stood everywhere. They ridiculed, spread confusion and threatened those who would stand for truth. But the walls were rebuilt by instituting the powerful Word of God. We can strengthen our world with a commitment to Jesus Christ, the King of kings, by His mighty name and by His mighty Word.

The Lord said, "If My people who are called by My name will humble themselves, and pray and seek My face, and turn from their wicked ways, then I will hear from heaven, and will forgive their sin and heal their land" (2 Chron. 7:14).

The winds of false doctrine have never blown harder or fiercer. As the momentum builds toward the return of the King of kings, the tension will increase. We need to be well aware of which words are from God and which are false.

If anyone teaches otherwise and does not consent to

wholesome words, even the words of our Lord Jesus Christ, and to the doctrine which accords with godliness, he is proud, knowing nothing, but is obsessed with disputes and arguments over words, from which come envy, strife, reviling, evil suspicions, useless wrangling of men of corrupt minds and destitute of the truth, who suppose that godliness is a means of gain. From such withdraw yourself.

—1 TIMOTHY 6:3–5

But evil men and imposters will grow worse and worse, deceiving and being deceived.

—2 TIMOTHY 3:13

SCRIPTURES FOR THE HEAT OF BATTLE

- "They will fight against you, but they shall not prevail against you" (Jer. 1:19).

- "The LORD shall go forth like a mighty man; He shall stir up His zeal like a man of war…He shall prevail against His enemies" (Isa. 42:13).

- "Be sober, be vigilant; because your adversary the devil walks about like a roaring lion, seeking whom he may devour. Resist him, steadfast in the faith, knowing that the same sufferings are experienced by your brotherhood in the world" (1 Pet. 5:8–9).

- "Therefore submit to God. Resist the devil and he will flee from you" (James 4:7).

- "Do not be afraid of their faces, for I am with you to deliver you" (Jer. 1:8).

- "If God is for us, who can be against us?" (Rom. 8:31).

- "God is faithful, who will not allow you to be tempted beyond what you are able, but with the temptation will also make a way of escape, that you may be able to bear it" (1 Cor. 10:13).

- "Have I not commanded you? Be strong and of good courage; do not be afraid, nor be dismayed, for the LORD your God is with you wherever you go" (Josh. 1:9).

- "Humble yourselves in the sight of the Lord, and He will lift you up" (James 4:10).

- "…striving together for the faith of the gospel, and not in any way terrified by your adversaries" (Phil. 1:27–28).

- "The words of the LORD are pure words, like silver tried in the furnace of the earth, purified seven times" (Ps. 12:6).

- "I will call upon the LORD, who is worthy to be praised; so shall I be saved from my enemies" (Ps. 18:3).

- "You prepare a table before me in the presence of my enemies" (Ps. 23:5).

- "Cast your burden on the LORD, and He shall sustain you; He shall never permit the righteous to be moved" (Ps. 55:22).

- "He will not be afraid of evil tidings; his heart is steadfast, trusting in the LORD. His heart is established; he will not be afraid until he sees his desire upon his enemies" (Ps. 112:7–8).

19

A Man of Peace

I have come as a light into the world, that whoever
believes in Me should not abide in darkness.

—John 12:46

Islam claims to be a religion of peace; it declares the
Qur'an as the final revelation and all other scriptures to
be bogus or obsolete. Such terminally deceptive peace
overtures are spouted daily in the media, but it must be
understood that Islamic peace is for Muslims only. All nonbelievers are to be placed into the House of War. Are there
are two different branches of Islam here, the one that
claims peace and the one that slammed into the World
Trade Center and the Pentagon? Which proponent can
marshal *jihad* to the greatest popular effect and define the
nature of conflict? Both recite the same prayers, conduct
the same rituals and aim their prayer rugs toward the city
of Mecca.

The Taliban are true believers in their ideology and policies, and they persistently invoke the will of Allah when
addressing the world. Their leader, Mullah Mohammad

Omar, has declared a *jihad* against America, Israel and the free world. Osama bin Laden's Al Qaeda network, blamed for conducting the suicide attacks in New York and Washington, also asks for divine blessing in waging *jihad*. In a videotape broadcast around the world, Osama bin Laden said, "As to America, I say to it and its people a few words: I swear to Allah that America will not live in peace before peace reigns in Palestine, and before all the army of infidels depart the land of Muhammad, peace be upon him."

It's essential to understand the two houses of Islam: *Dar el-Islam* (World of Islam) and the *Dar el-Harb* (World of War), where non-Muslim nations yet to be conquered are to be placed. The House of War gives Muslims the latitude to kill, steal and destroy in the name of Allah. In the law of Hudaibiya, Muhammad permitted Muslims to lie and break personal, business and political agreements with non-Muslims. Such spiritual counsel makes Islam a cross-cultural creed wearing a religious veil and a lethal exercise in horse-trading.

When Muslims speak of peace, the ideology is not what Westerners understand as peace. Islamic peace lasts only as long as the faithful are weaker than non-Muslims who do not embrace Allah and his prophet Muhammad. As soon as Muslims believe themselves to be stronger than their enemies, the Qur'an mandates they resume *jihad*, or holy war. In return for martyrdom, their families are compensated, their pictures are posted in schools and mosques, and they are promised unlimited sex with seventy-two virgins in heaven.[1] Indeed, this cruel lie has become hard currency in the extremist Muslim world.

Nonbelievers rejecting the Qur'an can face death. Initially, favorable Qur'anic verses were coined for nonbelievers, but after the Jews refused to fight with Muhammad and to accept him as their prophet, he fashioned verses for their total annihilation. As his follower

Yasir Arafat states, "Peace for us means the destruction of Israel, and nothing else."[2] Jamil Abu Bakr, a spokesman for the Jordanian Muslim Brotherhood, said, "Peace with Israel is inconceivable. How can there be peace? We are Muslims, and our holy book says Jews are our enemies."[3] America will be a similar target as long as she befriends Israel.

> Say to the Unbelievers, if (now) they desist (from unbelief), their past would be forgiven them; but if they persist, the punishment of those before them is already (a matter of warning for them). And fight them until there is no more tumult or oppression, and there prevail justice and faith in Allah altogether and everywhere.
>
> —SŪRAH 8:38–39

> Fight and slay the pagans wherever you find them and seize them, beleaguer them and lie in wait for them in every stratagem (of war).
>
> —SŪRAH 9:5

> Proclaim a grievous penalty to those who reject faith.
>
> —SŪRAH 9:3

Satan often comes as a subtle man of peace. Hitler constantly used the word *peace*, knowing full well that it is the shortest route to the hearts of enlightened democracies.[4] Muslims who strictly follow the Qur'an will not listen to those who want real peace, for the ultimate agenda is to destroy Israel and to nullify Jesus Christ as our Savior. Islam often wears white gloves concealing Satan's claws. The Bible warns, "Nor give place to the devil" (Eph. 4:27).

Saeed Hotari was a shy, devout young Muslim, a twenty-two-year-old young man of perceived peace, an electrician with boyish looks. One night in Tel Aviv he detonated a bomb in his clothing and killed twenty-one Israelis. His neighbors hung a picture of him holding seven sticks of dynamite on a tree. On a wall was spray-painted, "21 and counting." His father, Hassan Hotari, said, "I'm very happy and proud of what my son did and, frankly, a bit jealous. I wish I had done the bombing. My son has fulfilled Muhammad's wishes. He has become a hero! Tell me, what more could a father ask? My prayer is that Saeed's brothers, friends and fellow Palestinians will sacrifice their lives, too. There is no better way to show God you love him."[5]

Peace is the farthest thing from the Muslim fundamentalist's agenda. Signs on the walls of Hamas-run kindergartens read, "The children of the kindergarten are the *shaheeds* (holy martyrs) of tomorrow." The classroom signs at Al-Najah University in the West Bank and at Gaza's Islamic University say, "Israel has nuclear bombs; we have human bombs." At an Islamic school run by Hamas, eleven-year-old Ahmed's small frame and boyish smile are deceiving. They mask a determination to kill at any cost. "I will make my body a bomb that will blast the flesh of Zionists, the sons of pigs and monkeys," Ahmed says. "I will tear their bodies into little pieces and cause them more pain than they will ever know." "May the virgins give you pleasure," his teacher returns, referring to one of the rewards awaiting martyrs in paradise.

"You don't start educating a *shaheed* at age twenty-two," says Roni Shaked, a terrorism expert in Israel. "You start in kindergarten so by the time he's twenty-two, he's looking for an opportunity to sacrifice his life."[6]

Sheik Hasan Yosef claims that Palestinian children come up to him and say, "Conduct another bombing to make us happy, sheik." He answers, "I cannot disappoint them. They won't have to wait long." At any time, Israeli officials believe, Hamas has from five to twenty men, ages eighteen to twenty-three, awaiting orders to carry out suicide attacks. The group also claims to have tens of thousands of youths ready to follow in their footsteps. "We like to grow them," Yosef says, "from kindergarten through college." A would-be bomber is selected for his mission only days, sometimes hours, before it is to occur, Israeli officials say. As part of the preparation, the recruit is taken to a cemetery, where he is told to prepare for death by lying between gravesites for hours. He wears a white, hooded shroud normally used to cover bodies for burial, a former Hamas member says.[7]

The Bible says, "And do not fear those who kill the body but cannot kill the soul. But rather fear Him who is able to destroy both soul and body in hell" (Matt. 10:28). Proverbs tell us this fear is awe and reverence for God, and it is the beginning of wisdom (Prov. 9:10). Only Jesus can ultimately defeat the evil spirit of Islam.

> For we do not wrestle against flesh and blood, but against principalities, against powers, against the rulers of the darkness of this age, against spiritual hosts of wickedness in the heavenly places.
> —EPHESIANS 6:12

The hope of all Christians is that Muslims will realize that they are not only fighting against America, Israel and the free world, but that they are actually fighting against God's truth as revealed in Bible.

Muslims indeed must find the Prince of Peace, the Son of God who became flesh and blood and died for everyone without protest, for Jesus so loves the world.

> The Lord is not slack concerning His promise, as some count slackness, but is longsuffering toward us, not willing that any should perish but that all should come to repentance.
> —2 PETER 3:9

Jesus stood in our stead to destroy evil. "The thief does not come except to steal, and to kill, and to destroy. I have come that they may have life, and that they may have it more abundantly" (John 10:10). My prayer is that mankind will find peace, that no one, whether by spirit or force, loses the peace and love that surpasses all understanding in Christ Jesus.

By cultivating intense hostility, by teaching children to hate and by the constant preparations for a war of annihilation, Muslim extremists continue to plague the earth, but they only prevent the blessings in store for them. All Muslims must choose with courage between peace or forging Islam into a battle sword, between eternal destruction or eternal blessings. Jesus loves all Muslims. Jesus loves Osama bin Laden. It is up to the Christian to make the love of Jesus visible. There is a solution to this mad confusion. Christians must lift up Jesus.

> And I, if I am lifted up from the earth, will draw all peoples to Myself.
>
> —JOHN 12:32

GLOSSARY

Alhamdullillah: Praise be to Allah

Al-Kitab-ul Muqaddas: The Bible

Allah: The name of the creator of the universe

Allahu Akbar: Allah is greater than anything else

Al-Quds: Jerusalem

Allah Subhana wa Ta'ala: God the glorified and exalted

Allah Ta'ala: God Most High

Al-Tawrat: The Book of Moses (Torah)

Al-Zabur: The Psalms of David

Asr: Late afternoon prayer

As-salamu alai kum: Greeting: "Peace be upon you"

Ayah: Verse in the Qur'an

Bidah: Innovated practices introduced into the Islamic religion

Bismillah: "In the name of Allah"; usually invoked before a lawful practice

Bismillah-ir Rahman-ir Rahim: "In the name of Allah the Merciful, the Compassionate"

Dajjal: Antichrist

Daud and Sulaiman: David and Solomon

Dawah: Propogation of Islam through word and deed, calling people to follow the commands of Allah

Deen: A comprehensive word that usually means religion or a way of life following the dictates of Muhammad

Eid Al Fitr: Three-day festival marking the end of Ramadan, the month of fasting

Eid Al Adha: Four-day feast of sacrifice commemorating the Prophet Ibrahim's obedience to Allah by being willing to sacrifice his only son Ishmael

Fajr: Early morning prayer

Fatiha: The opening chapter of the Qur'an and to be read with every prayer

Ghusl: Full ritual washing of the body with water; should be done after intercourse, wet dreams, emission, menses and childbirth

Hadith: Saying and traditions of the prophet Muhammad

Hajj: Pilgrimage to the Holy City of Mecca

Hijab: Veil worn by Muslim women for reasons of modesty and protection

Hijjah: The last Islamic month

Imam: Leads prayer; also a scholar

Iman: Truth, faith, acceptance

Injil Sharif: New Testament (Gospel)

Isa: Arabic for Jesus

Isa Al-Masih: Jesus the Messiah

Isha: Night prayer

Ishaq and Yaqub: Isaac and Jacob

Islam: Literally means submission to Allah

Ismail: Ishmael

Jahanam: Hell

Jannah: Paradise

Jibreel: Angel Gabriel

Jihad: Holy war to establish the Islamic way of life

Jinn: A race of created beings made out of smokeless fire

Juma: Friday; the Muslim day for gathering on Friday noon prayers

Kaba: Holiest shrine constructed for the worship of Allah; Muslims face in this direction

Kafir: An unbeliever to be converted or killed

Khalifa: A Muslim ruler of an Islamic state

Khutba: Sermon

Maghrib: Sunset prayer

Malaikah: Angels

Maryam: Mary

Maseeh: A title of anointed given to Jesus

Masjid: Mosque or place of worship

Muhammad: The name of the final messenger and prophet of Allah to humanity

Muharram: The first month of the Islamic calendar

Musa and Harun: Moses and Aaron

Muslim: Literally means submission to Allah

Nabi: Prophet

Qibla: Direction all Muslims face during prayer

Quoran: The last revelation of Allah to Muhammad through the angel Gabriel

Rabb-ul A`alamin: Lord of Heaven and Earth (the Universe)

Ramadan: Month of fasting, the ninth month of the Islamic calendar

Sahabi: Companion of prophet Muhammad

Sajda: Prostration, as in prayer

Saum: Fasting

Shahada: The creed of Islam: "I bear witness that there is no deity but Allah and Muhammad is his messenger"

Shaitan: Satan

Shar'ia: Islamic law, encompassing the Qur'an and Hadith, the sayings of the prophet Muhammad

Shirk: Associating partners with Allah; grave sin is not to forgive a person if he dies in that state

Subhan Allah: "Glory be to Allah"

Suhuf-un Nabiyin: Writings of the Prophets

Sürah: Chapter in the Qur'an

Tahara: Purification of the body clothing and souls

Tawheed: The divine unity, in its most profound sense; Allah is one in his essence and his attributes and his acts

Taymmum: Dry purification when water is not available or is detrimental to health

Ummra: A pilgrimage to Mecca

Wa alai kum as-salam: Return greeting: "And peace be upon you"

Witr: A prayer that has odd number of *rakat* (units); usually referred to the last prayer of the night after the Isha prayer

Wudu: Purifying with water before performing prayers

Yahya: John the Baptist

NOTES

Chapter 1
Antichrist

1. Sahih Muslim, Book 40, #6985.
2. Malik, *The Quranic Concept of War*, 59–60.
3. Hadith Tirmzi, Vol. 1, 417.
4. William Harwood, *Mythology's Last Gods: Yahweh and Jesus* (n.p.: Prometheus Books, 1992), 248.
5. Ibne Majah, Vol. 2, 166.

Chapter 4
Islam's Advent

1. William Goldsack, *Muhammad in Islam* (Madras, India: n.p., 1916), 12.
2. *Great Religions of the World* (n.p.: National Geographic Society, 1971), 227.

Chapter 6
The Question of Which Angel

1. Abd-al-Masih, *Who Is Allah in Islam?* (n.p.: n.d.), 68.

Chapter 7
Women of Islam

1. Hadith Tirmzi, vol. 2, 35-40; vol. 3, 83-97, 138.
2. Ayatollah Khomeini Tahrirolvasyleh, Vol. 4 (Darol Elm, Gom, Iran: 1990).
3. *Sayings of Ayatollah Khomeini, Political, Phylosophica, Social and Religious*, with a special introduction by Clive Irving (n.p.: n.d.), 47.
4. Burnham al-Din al-Marghinani, *Al-Hidaya* (London: 1870), 25–32.

Chapter 8
Basic Islam

1. *Seattle Times* (April 9, 1989).

Chapter 9
A War Called Jihad

1. Alfred Guillaume, *The Life of Muhammad* (London: Oxford University Press, 1955), 205.
2. J. Murdock, *Arabia and Its Prophet* (n.p.: 1922), 20.
3. Guillaume, *The Life of Muhammad*, 369.
4. Sunan of Abu Dawud, Book 19, No. 2996.
5. A. J. Wensinak, *Muhammad and the Jews of Medina* (n.p.: n.d.), 113.
6. Guillaume, *The Life of Muhammad*, 675.
7. *Time* (February 27, 1989): 33.
8. Ibid., 28–33.
9. Leila S. Kadi, *Basic Political Documents* (Beruit: PLO Research Center, 1969), 137–142.
10. Yossi Melman, *The Master Terrorist: The True Story of Abu-Nidal* (n.p.: Adama Books, 1986), 77.
11. David Lamb, *The Arabs* (New York: Random House, 1987), 287.

Chapter 10
Islam's Outward Face

1. Martin Lings, *Muhammad: His Life Based on the Earliest Sources* (London: Inner Traditions International Ltd., 1983), 9.

Chapter 12
Sufism

1. A Nicholson, *Legacy of Islam* (London: 1939), 218.

2. Abu Nu'aym al-Isfahani, hilyat al-Awliya, Vol. II (Cairo: 1933), 132.

Chapter 14
Jesus, a Mere Man?

1. Josh McDowell, *More Than a Carpenter* (Wheaton, IL: Tyndale House, 1987), 61–62.

Chapter 15
Why Israel?

1. *Issues: A Messianic Jewish Perspective*, Volume 10, 2.

2. Sahih Muslim, Book 40, #6985.

3. Adapted from "Converging Destinies: Jerusalem, Peace and the Messiah," accessed via the Internet at http://answering-islam.org.uk/peacemaker.html.

4. *Christian Jew Newsletter*, Charles Halff

5. Ibid.

6. *Issues*, 2.

7. Jacob Jocz, *A Theology of Election: Israel and the Church* (New York: 1958), 106.

Chapter 17
Israel and Jesus Today

1. *Issues*, 5.

Chapter 19
A Man of Peace

1. Sürah 78:31.

2. Vitalij Raevskij, "Yasir Arafat: The Biography of the Terrorist," *Shalom* 208 (November 1999).

3. Associated Press news, 1/3/00.

4. Oriana Falaci, *Interview With History* (Boston: Hougthon Mifflin Company, 1976).

5. From Jack Kelly, "Devotion, Desire Drives Youth to Martyrdom," *USA Today* (July 5, 2001).

6. Ibid.

7. Ibid.

BIBLIOGRAPHY

Browne, E. G., P. R. E. Browne and E. M. A. Browne. *Literary History of Persia*. N.p.: n.d.

Goldsack, William. *Muhammad in Islam*. Madras, India: 1916.

Guilluame, Alfred. *The Life of Muhammad*. London: Oxford University Press, 1955.

Lings, Martin. *Muhammad: His Life Based on the Earliest Sources*. London: Inner Traditions International Ltd., 1983.

Melman, Yossi. *The Master Terrorist: The True Story of Abu-Nidal*. Adama Books: 1986.

Padivick, Constantine, S.B.C.K. *Muslim Devotions*. N.p.: n.d.

Parrinder, Edward Geoffrey. *World Religions, From Ancient Heritage to the Present*. New York: Hamlyn Publishers Group, n.d.

Williams, John Walden and George Brazziler. *Islam*. New York: 1983.

If you enjoyed *Jesus vs. Jihad*, here are some other titles
from Charisma House that we think will minister to you...

Inside Islam
Reza Safa
ISBN: 0-88419-416-7
Retail Price: $13.99

Author Reza Safa, a former Shiite Muslim, exposes the spirit of
Islam from an insider's point of view. Safa is well versed in the laws
and history of Islam, but more importantly, he brings to light the
corrupt agenda of this destructive global force.

The Missions Addiction
David Shibley
ISBN: 0-88419-772-7
Retail Price: $13.99

In these action-packed pages, you will discover a Global Jesus
Generation that is creating discomfort in the church and change in
missions worldwide. God is calling you to become part of a conta-
gious epidemic of missions-hearted believers who will bring global
fame to His name!

Married to Muhammed
W. L. Cati
A Creation House Press Imprint
ISBN: 0-88419-794-8
Retail Price: $10.99

In this eye-opening exposé of the often deceptive tactics Muslims
use to gain converts, W. L. Cati warns women of the dangers of dat-
ing and marrying Islamic men. Through original Muslim writings
and a chilling account of her own fourteen-year marriage to a
Muslim, Cati sheds light on the dark side of Islam—especially the
teachings and practices that keep women in suffocating bondage.

Charisma®
HOUSE
Books about Spirit-Led Living

To pick up a copy of any of these titles, contact
your local Christian bookstore or order online
at www.charismawarehouse.com.